How To Become An Efficient Manager

S.K. Tarafder

ATLANTIC
PUBLISHERS & DISTRIBUTORS (P) LTD

Published by

ATLANTIC

PUBLISHERS & DISTRIBUTORS (P) LTD

7/22, Ansari Road, Darya Ganj,
New Delhi-110002
Phones : +91-11-23273880, 23275880, 23280451
Fax : +91-11-23285873
Web : www.atlanticbooks.com
E-mail : info@atlanticbooks.com

Branch Office
5, Nallathambi Street, Wallajah Road,
Chennai-600002
Phones : +91-44-64611085, 32413319
E-mail : chennai@atlanticbooks.com

Printed in India at Nice Printing Press, A-33/3A, Site-IV, Industrial Area, Sahibabad, Ghaziabad, U.P.

Preface

Managers are the pillars of organisations. With the privatisation policy of the Government of India, the number of organisations under the management of private ownership is on the increase, and in order to take such organisations to the zenith of efficiency, competent managers are the need of the day.

This book titled, *How To Become An Efficient Manager* is a very useful book for the working managers as well as for those who have the innate inclination to become managers of organisations in their future career. This book dwells upon practical aspects on a number of matters which the managers ought to know in order to fertilise their working with utmost efficiency and zeal. Efficient managers are the crying need of the day and they will derive maximum benefits to enrich their knowledge of working through perusal of this book. By virtue of my practical experience which I have gleaned by working in senior managerial capacity for sixteen years with the organisations of All-India repute, I have given pragmatic views for the benefit of the managers who have a keen desire to be fully successful in their career. Through questions and answers

I have also discussed many important issues which the persons working in managerial capacity are required to know for the efficient functioning of the organisations with which they are associated and for their own career development as well.

Throughout the book, I have used masculine gender, such as 'He/Manager' without mentioning feminine gender, such as 'She/Manageress'. I beg apology from the female readers of this book for not mentioning feminine gender as I have used masculine gender for the purpose of ease in writing.

S.K. Tarafder

Contents

Who are Managers?

1

Customary definition of Manager is that the person who acts to manage the affairs of the organisation is a Manager. Managers of organisations have to instil in them the managerial qualities needed to justify performance of official members in consonance with their designation. Excellent Managers are those who prove equal to the task. Managers are the inviolable and solid pillars of organisations on which depend the prosperity of the establishments where they work. Competent Managers are the essence of rejuvenating the economic morbidity of the establishments steering clear the obstacles standing in the way of development of such organisations. While efficient running of organisations stimulates generation of employment potentiality, Managers have to play a great role in solving unemployment problem by making the organisations economically viable by their indefatigable working.

Needless to elucidate, country's development depends largely upon the efficient Managers who are the guiding force to mould the economy of the country to the betterment by way of efficient running of organisations, which is the absolute need of the day. Managers have to realise always that they are engaged not only for the sake of normal discharge of their duties but also for broader perspective and that they have immense and perennial responsibilities to shoulder being placed in Managerial position.

Managers must have creative instincts with a managerial perspective and skill. There won't also be any dearth of expert advice from them. Managers should be acquainted with organisational behaviour. They should also need to deal with the time orientation of employees as they attempt to compete through speed. The temporal perspective work-teams become an important issue for the Managers to bear in mind when cooperation among several departments is required or is essential for performance of tasks. Moreover, the Managers cannot ignore the human element while managing a company.

The following chapters have elaborately dealt with the aspects as to how to become a successful Manager. "Success is the progressive realisation of a worthy goal"—says Earl Nightingale.

Personality of a Manager

2

A Manager must possess good personality. It is one of the most important factors on which depends the success of a Manager. Personality is an essential ingredient need to be maintained by a successful Manager throughout the period of his service career. Personality does not mean that a Manager is essentially required to be good looking which alone will not suffice the purpose entirely. Appearance in fact is considered to determine personality of a Manager, when a Manager has to work in the office along with his co-officers and subordinate staff members, his personality will go a long way in maintaining rapprochement with them in the interest of smooth working and here lies the success of a Manager. A Manager with good personality is liked by everybody who feels closed to him. This is his added qualification in the discharge of his duties efficiently in communion with them. Now, after discussing in the foregoing all about the personality, the question naturally crops up what are the traits of good personality. Good personality is the embodiment of the following traits.

(a) Self-confidence

(b) Fixity of mind

(c) Capacity to influence others

(d) Clarity of expression

(e) Not to be fickle minded

(f) Capacity of quick understanding

(g) Wearing of well fitted costume

(h) Positive approach on matters

(i) Cleanliness

(j) Gravity
(k) Steadiness in walking
(l) Sense of etiquette
(m) Good manners
(n) Will power
(o) Gentleness
(p) Soft spoken
(q) Cool temperament
(r) Good behaviour
(s) Loveable habits.

Explanations of the above traits seriatim are the following:

Self-confidence

Since a Manager has to shoulder higher responsibilities in the discharge of his duties, he should have self-confidence for attaining perfection in the job he does. Therefore, for a successful Manager self-confidence is an absolute necessity.

Fixity of mind

A Manager has to take multifarious decisions in the interest of the organisation he serves for. Therefore, he has to think twice before arriving at a final decision. Otherwise, it may be detrimental to the interest of the organisation and the Manager taking such decision will be held entirely responsible for the same. Hence, fixity of mind of a successful Manager is a prerequisite so as to avoid swinging of decisions which will speak of the unsteady mind of the Manager. Unsteady mind is a disqualification to become a successful Manager.

Capacity to influence others

Getting jobs done by influencing others is the yard-stick of a successful Manager. For attaining this art he has to be amiable in disposition, choleric disposition of the Manager will ruffle others and the jobs cannot be got done by him by influencing them. This will be his disqualification and will go against his personality. Therefore, a Manager has to cultivate the art of influencing others.

Clarity of expression

Clarity of expression is a part of personality of a Manager, with clarity of expression of the Manager the employees do not feel confused to understand things he explains to them and the jobs are done by them efficiently and without error.

Not to be fickle minded

Fickle mindedness is a great weakness of a Manager, with fickle mindedness the employees do not, in fact, treat him with respect and when respectability is wanting discipline in the organisation cannot be upheld. Higher management will also try to get rid of such fickle minded Manager.

Capacity of quick understanding

One of the ingredients of a successful Manager is that he should have the capacity of quick understanding of things which will help him perform his duties with promptitude and dexterity. Quick understanding of things will also conduce him to work against time thus instilling efficiency in the working of the Manager.

Wearing of well fitted costume

A Manager must be well dressed. This will enhance Company's prestige. Wearing of well fitted costume with proper dressing of hair brings smartness which reflects in the working.

Positive approach on matters

A successful Manager is a person who has positive approach on matters. Negative approach retards progress of work and the work of the Manager goes on piling up for such negative approach and ultimately he becomes a failure in the discharge of his duties.

Cleanliness

Propensity for inculcating cleanliness is a virtue. This brings perfection in the working of a Manager.

Gravity

Gravity is a very important part to become a successful Manager. Employees treat the Manager with gravity in high esteem.

Steadiness in walking

Steadiness in walking by a Manager reflects the promptness of his action on every matter.

Sense of etiquette

A Manager must have sense of etiquette. It shows elegance of his mind which otherwise means that he is a man of good taste. Elegance and highness of mind is the essence of a successful Manager.

Good manners

A Manager possessing good manners is a person hailing from aristocratic family. Successful Managers are those who come of respectable families. Family background is very important for a person to become a Manager because his attitude is moulded on the basis of his family environment.

Will power

A Manager having will power is indomitable and such indomitable Manager is a strong pillar for the organisation, who can face any ordeal bravely and successfully that may come up during the course of his working. His will power will help him acquire further higher position in the organisation.

Gentleness

The essence of a successful Manager is gentleness. His gentle habits make him loveable amongst the employees.

Soft spoken

A successful Manager must be soft spoken. Speaking in loud voice by a Manager disturbs others in their working and also it does not speak high of the Manager. Well polished Manager is always soft spoken. When a Manager is soft spoken, others will also follow suit and the company's work continues in peaceful atmosphere. Pandemonium is contradictory to peaceful working.

Cool temperament

A successful Manager must have cool temperament always. Since he is saddled with plenty of work at his disposal, it is essentially desired that his cool temperament will go a long way in solving the knotty problems. A Manager with ruffled temperament complicates matters and the company has to suffer a lot for his immature decision which owes for his intemperance. Therefore, cool temperament is the essence of a successful Manager.

Good behaviour

Devotion to duties by the employees is the result of good behaviour of the Manager. It is the psychological effect of cool behaviour of the Manager that the employees are inspired to do more work without whiling away their time. By this way, the company gets benefit arising out of the increased output of work performed by the employees.

Loveable habits

Loveable habits of the Manager draw the employees closer to him in the discharge of duties. Extraction of work from the employees by showing red eyes is primitive. Work through love and affection as shown by the Manager is the go of the modern times. By such way of working formation of labour union in the organisation is also a remote possibility.

It is, therefore, of utmost importance that the Manager desiring to be successful in his working, has to abide by the above traits which are absolutely indispensible.

Academic Qualification of a Manager

3

Excellent academic qualification is not the absolute criterion to become a Manager of a company. If we take into account that only those persons are eligible to become the Managers having high degree of academic education, it is a mistaken conception. Everybody is not fortunate to prosecute studies to acquire high degree of academic education because of multiple reasons, and it has been observed that such persons are also competent Managers. While it is an admitted fact that persons with excellent academic qualifications are eligible to become Managers by virtue of their harnessing with sufficient knowledge so acquired through such education, many persons have also managerial capability and competence with lesser academic qualification not equalising with those having high degree of academic qualification.

In this connection, it will be appropriate to analyse what is education in true sense of the term. If any person has the ability to choose between wisdom and foolishness and between good and bad irrespective of academic degrees, they are called educated persons. Such educated persons can also become Managers having value based education, mental acumen and intelligence with which they are able to understand things quickly and sort out problems, whatever difficult the same may be.

Even without excellent academic qualification a person could be successful in his every effort if he is in possession of conviction, courage, courtesy, character and commitment.

Many of the Managers must have all the above principles even when they are not highly academically educated.

Intelligence and ability are also other traits of a person facilitating him to become a Manager although he may not have high degree of academic qualification. Intelligence helps quicken to learn and ability is the skill to apply what is learnt. Knowledge is something which can also be acquired without high degree of academic qualification, and this knowledge could be fully utilised by the Manager during the course of his working. Knowledge is information which is a potential power and this power is the most essential power required by a Manager.

From the above analyses it is construed that high degree of academic qualification is not necessarily required in all the cases to become a successful Manager in a Company provided he can develop the required traits to work as Manager. There is of course no denying the fact that the highly educated persons with speciality in commercial and management degrees are by far competent to become Managers and the importance of such persons in commercial world is immense.

4

Taking Judicious and Prompt Action and Having Capacity to Surmise Reaction to the Action Taken by a Manager

An efficient Manager should not take delatory action of any matter. He should never swing to take action as it speaks ill of his working competence. Certain actions to be taken by a competent Manager are of course urgent and immediate. Such actions must, therefore, be taken without any delay, else the situation may be out of control. It is to be remembered that some decisions to be taken may be complex. In such case, gathering more information before arriving at a decision is of vital necessity, which should be done at the quickest possible time. If necessary, taking into account the gravity and complexity of the situation, consultation with the top management of the organisation could be made and their advice taken in the matter. Right decision could be taken in less time if a decision-making process is used. A Manager may have number of decisions to be taken and it may not be necessary to take all the decisions at a time, in this case, he has to prepare a comprehensive list of the matters against which the decisions are to be taken, which should be done on the basis of priority. A competent Manager should study all aspects in true perspective before taking any judicious action so that the organisation where he has been working is not put to jeopardy for taking hasty and immature decision.

A Manager must have the capacity to surmise reaction to the action taken by him, because he must be well aware of the fact that every action has got reaction. Reckless and immature action taken by a Manager without conjecturing the complications which emanate out of the same will put him in awkward situation as also the company where he serves. Moreover, for such immature action taken by him his services with the company may even be at stake. It is, therefore, of paramount necessity that a judicious Manager must think twice before taking a final action, so that the reaction to the same does not become detrimental to the interest of the organisation as also his position as Manager. A Manager is part and parcel of an organisation. His deeds and actions are important in upholding the prestige of the organisation. Matured action taken by a Manager speaks high of his competence.

Since a Manager is one of the pillars of the organisation, he cannot shirk of his responsibilities to the organisation and being a responsible Manager he has to take action instantly at times of exigency of circumstances and in such case he has to be meticulous to take judicious action in the interest of the organisation on the basis of his mental make-up and maturity of thought so that such action does not have any adverse effect. If the Manager is swinging in his action it proves of his incompetence to work as Manager. Therefore, in order to become a competent and successful Manager he must be alert to take appropriate action on any matter and this will prove his capacity to surmise reaction to the action taken by him.

For the purpose of taking judicious action so that its reaction does not impair the prestige of the organisation, a Manager needs assessment of his risk-taking ability and in this connection analyses of his strengths, weaknesses, opportunities and threats (SWOT) are essential.

5

How should a Manager Work?

After the days work a Manager should feel confident that the job he has accomplished is completely under his control. This will make him worry-free after he returns home and that his mind will not be tormented. He can, therefore, start his work next day in the office with renewed vigour, strength and interest, as there will not be piling up of any work barring aside a few awaiting completion. He should always keep his work environment tidy, which will make him jovial. A Manager should keep in mind the following aspects.

(a) He should respond to all incoming communications immediately,

(b) He should keep his work environment tidy,

(c) He should know exactly what are his objectives,

(d) He should know what actions need to be done first,

(e) He should take decisions at the right time,

(f) He should deal with matters that are important before they become urgent,

(g) He should keep the structure of filing system up-to-date,

(h) He should keep a good balance between work and leisure.

Responsibility of a Manager and its Effect on the Employees

6

Under no circumstances, a Manager can shirk from his responsibilities in the discharge of his duties. There is a saying, Responsibilities gravitate to the person who can shoulder them. When a Manager accepts responsibility he is actually giving himself promotion. A Manager who is away from shouldering responsibilities is of course not set free from being responsible. When he thinks himself responsible he can take judicious actions during the course of his working. Responsibility involves thoughtful action. There is maturity of thoughts and actions of a Manager when he is responsible in his behaviour. It is the general tendency of human being that when things go wrong he does not want to accept responsibility. But, when things go right he takes the credit whether he has taken responsibility for the same or not. But, in the case of a Manager this should not be made applicable. He must be bold to accept that he is responsible for things going wrong and here lies his credibility. By this, the higher management of the organisation will not nurture the opinion that such a Manager is an opportunist and at the same time he will enjoy respectability from all for his bold confession of folly. A responsible Manager is no doubt a successful and trustworthy Manager. The price of greatness is responsibility. Shouldering responsibility by a Manager is his moral obligation.

Effect of responsibility of a Manager on the employees

The effect of his being responsible is that the subordinate employees can learn from him as to how they have to cultivate the habit of generating sense of responsibility which will pave the way for their future prosperity in service. Irresponsibility of a person is a degeneration. An irresponsible Manager cannot have control over his staff members, because he cannot remain firm and steady in the eyes of the employees and consequently they do not discharge their duties with care and responsibility taking cue of the irresponsibility of their Manager. A responsible Manager is a strong pillar of an organisation. The employees will feel elated when they work under a responsible Manager. Responsibility brings discipline. The employees are made disciplined when they work through discipline which is the aftermath of the responsible way of working of the Manager under whom they work. Instances are plenty that many employees have ascended the ladder of higher position in service because of the high degree of training they received by virtue of their working under a competent and responsible Manager and this has become their asset throughout the period of their service career.

Creativity of Ideas of a Manager

7

The ability to think creatively is an essential ingredient for every competent Manager. By this, he will understand the process of generating and assessing ideas. This will also help him find innovative solutions to difficult problems. Creative people have provided new solutions to the problems. In organisations, creativity is essential to ensure a firm's ongoing effectiveness in a changing world. A Manager has to think creatively to increase his opportunities. He should use his past experience to find solutions. By his relevant experience he can choose the most appropriate path and move towards a solution, creative thinking of a Manager involves opening up his mind to find new solutions and new ways of doing things. A Manager has to bear in mind that imagination is the life-blood of creativity. In order to be more creative he should be aware of how he usually responds to situations or issues. For developing creativity he needs to overcome the natural barriers in his mind which is very important. Needless to mention, new ideas and creativity are essential for progress.

Thinking creatively by a Manager helps him find ways to deal with challenges. A creative Manager provides new solutions to the problems. There is generation of ideas by thinking creatively. By his creativity he must be open-minded in his approach to situations. He should always try to cope with his workload by finding creative ways to work more efficiently. Important fact is that he has to overcome the natural barriers in his mind in order to succeed in developing his innate creativity. Creativity is also stimulated when ideas are shared with other colleagues. A Manager has to examine how the creative process works and start to change his current patterns of thinking. He should be humourous. This will provide analogy to his creative process. By his creativity he should be ready to adapt his attitude to suit different occasions.

8

Instilling Team Spirit and Developing Motivation amongst the Employees

One of the factors determining the success of a Manager is how he is able to infuse team spirit and ignite motivation amongst the employees. Team work accentuates progress of work in an organisation. Work cannot be extracted from the employees by coercive methods adopted by a Manager. A Manager must take into account the performance of the working group or team which will have the effect of team spirit. This makes for greater accountability. It also encourages cooperation amongst co-workers. In the new dispensation, team players have the edge. Today, overall corporate performance is also a factor.

Apart from instilling team spirit a Manager has also to encourage generation of motivation by the employees which is very important to attain dexterity in the working of the organisation. Motivation means to turn on or ignite the feeling or action. Motivation is a driving force. It can persuade and propel the employees into action. In other words, motivation can be defined as motive for action. It is a force that can transform life.

Now, the question is: can the Manager motivate the employees? The answer must be in the negation. The thing is that it is the employees who motivate themselves and not the others who can motivate them. A Manager has, of course, to inspire them to motivate themselves. He can create conducive environment which can be motivating. In order to inspire the employees to motivate themselves, a Manager has to understand their sentiments, needs and wants. The difference between inspiration and motivation is that inspiration is changing thinking; motivation is changing action.

Success of a Manager will depend upon his taking the following actions and then only the employees will have sense of team spirit and motivation.

(a) A Manager should treat the employees in such a way that they are not made to feel that they have no status in the organisation,

(b) Human mind is very much sensitive. Therefore, a Manager should not hurt the sentiment of the employees by taking such action or talking with them in irrational way,

(c) He should treat all the employees with equal eyes. Feelings of nepotism and favouritism should not dawn in the minds of a Manager,

(d) He should have soft corner in his mind to understand the genuine problems and difficulties of the employees,

(e) Previously, there was the concept of master and servant relations in the office. But, now this concept has changed altogether as employee-employer relations. Although a Manager is a Management staff, yet his relations with the employees will be very sweet and cordial in view of the changed situation in modern day employment,

(f) A Manager at the same time should not show laxity while dealing with the erring employees, else his administration will fail and that he will be an unsuccessful Manager,

(g) He should listen to what the employees say,

(h) He should give recognition to the services of the employees.

While inspiring the employees to motivate themselves, a Manager should be well aware of what are the factors by which the employees are demotivated. They are:

(a) Unfair and negative criticism,

(b) Humiliation to the employees,

(c) Disregarding self-esteem to the employees,

(d) Bad office politics.

Writing Skill of a Manager 9

Effective communication through writing is essential for a Manager who wants to progress in today's business environments. Such communication is a valuable equipment to help meet any challenge which may crop up while working in a business establishment. All business communications benefit from a straightforward writing style. Business letters should not be lengthy else the readers will feel irksome and boring to read such letters. Basic requirements for effective written communications are: clear and concise style, knowledge of grammar and structure, avoiding verbose style English and how to apply basic formats to everyday communication. Knowledge of efficient communication in the field of employment has enormous advantage knowledge, training, education, organisational skills and creativity of Manager are reflected in the words he uses in his letters. Through his way of writing a Manager can gain confidence by the recipients of his letters. Writing positively and directly can influence others. It is recommended that for electronic communications a Manager should always write to the point and in simple language, so that the readers can understand things properly through the communications written by the Manager.

It is the quality of writing that is important. The fact is that if a communication is badly written, it will not promote clear understanding by the recipients. Well-written letters are always interesting to read. A good writing style has several different elements. It should give a positive message, show the writer's familiarity with the subject matter, convey the right information in a concise and friendly manner and, if necessary, motivate the readers. The style and tone that the Manager uses in his writing project his image and can also reflect his credibility in the workplace. Before writing letters a Manager has to first assimilate points in mind and then dictate to his Personal Assistant/Private Secretary to type out in the form of letters/reports, in doing so, the Manager has not to pause number of times while dictating letters/reports, thus saving lot of time which could be fruitfully utilised for doing other important work at his disposal. It is important to mention that some complicated/policy matter letters or reports should be typed out in draft form so that some additions/alterations could be done before typing them finally.

Courtesy and Manners

10

Success of a person depends upon courtesy and manners. Instances are plenty that many talented persons have failed to attain their own success because they are derelect of courtesy and manners. A man of courtesy and manners is a man of refined temperament and politeness which are the hallmark of gentleness. Courtesy and good manners enhance the self-growth of a person. It costs nothing to be courteous but pays a lot not only to the individual but to the organisation too. A man of courtesy and good manners is loveable by all and sundry. He does not have any foe. A man of towering personality is one endowed with the virtue of courtesy and manners. Such person is elevated in the eyes of others.

A Manager in an organisation must be a person of qualities, it is of paramount necessity that a Manager must be a person of courtesy and manners. Otherwise, his success as Manager will have retrograde step. While a Manager without courtesy and manners is not liked by others, he will not be able to imprint good impressions in the minds of the officials/executives of other organisations also, and that he will find it difficult to get the job done of which he is entrusted with.

Gentleness and politeness of a Manager enhance the prestige, honour and reputation of an organisation where he serves. A Manager with ruffled and choleric disposition is derelect of courtesy and manners which is his negative point to become a Manager. Good manners and courteous behaviour of a Manager bring the employees close to him which is very much conducive to generate team spirit in working. This obviously leads to prosperity of the organisation in the long run.

Manager's contribution is immense for the well-being of an organisation when he is a person of courtesy and manners which play an important part for him to become a successful Manager. Job of a Manager is as such that he has to face many obstacles and ordeals during the course of his working. His success is measured in terms when he has done the jobs well by overcoming the impediments. He will of course feel plain sailing in getting success in his jobs when he will be assisted by his employees and co-officers in most of the cases because of his amiable and loveable habits which he has acquired by his courtesy and manners.

Leadership Qualities of a Manager

11

Everybody cannot be a responsible and successful Manager unless otherwise he has the leadership qualities. If a person has strong inclination to rise high in service he can think of developing leadership qualities. Leadership qualities drive a person to reach the highest echelon of life. It all depends upon how a person is enthusiastic. Enthusiasm breeds a person to become energetic. A successful Manager must be energetic. In all the cases, leadership qualities are not inborn. The leadership qualities of a Manager are:

(a) He should have sound knowledge of work,

(b) He should distribute work in such a way that the employees are not overburdened, otherwise the work cannot be done by them with perfection,

(c) All the employees should be made to feel that they are part and parcel of the organisation,

(d) He should treat all the employees with equal eyes,

(e) He must have patience,

(f) He should not utter any unparliamentary words which will injure the hearts of the employees.

(g) He should have good rapprochement with other officers of the organisation,

(h) He should be bold enough to take decision,

(i) He should discipline the employees,

(j) He should inspire and encourage the employees,

(k) He should not lose temper on any occasion,

(l) He should listen to what the subordinates say and try to solve their problems,

(m) There should not be any sense of favourtism in him,

(n) He should not criticise any employee,

(o) He should have the capability to study the behavioural pattern and psychology of the employees,

(p) He should maintain cordial relations with the employees,

(q) He must maintain punctuality in attending office to set example for others,

(r) He should not tolerate any laxity in the performance to work by the employees,

(s) He should understand and realise the genuine difficulties and problems of the employees,

(t) He should have fore-sightedness, i.e. he must conjecture what may be the repercussion after he takes action on any matter, because every action has reaction.

The Art of Influencing Others

12

A Manager should have power to influence others by his artifice. Powers of persuation contribute directly to his ability to achieve his goals. Persuation is defined as the ability to convince others to accept the ideas of the influencer. The Manager can win people's hearts when he respects their sentiments and aspirations. In order to convince the people of the merits of a proposal, he needs to demonstrate how his ideas meet their needs. A Manager should understand that effective influence stems from two-way dialogue. A competent Manager works with others to create agreements, build relationships and achieve results. Before he can satisfy mutual goals, he needs to be clear about his own goals. Before he introduces himself to someone, he should think about what he wants from the contact. In order to enable him to work with efficiency he should gain rapport, avoid fruitless conflict and create mutual respects. A Manager should keep in mind that he should not be rigid in his attitude but should be easy and frank which will help him influence his colleagues. Another distinguishing feature is that the ability of the Manager to persuade others rests upon how he presents a well-argued and logical case supported by evidence. He should make his arguments attractive. A Manager has to build reputation for trustworthiness, keeping his promises and supporting others when they are in difficulty. If mistrust has taken place, he should bury the hatchet by making amends for his own mistakes. It is necessary to secure agreement from his senior

Managers in respect of his proposals. He should impress upon his senior Managers with his ability to handle responsibility.

13

Keeping Normalcy in Dealing with Spate of Work

Patience is a great virtue and a moral excellence of a Manager, by virtue of which he can overcome problems volley after volley. A Manager has to pass through spate of work. But he is not to be ruffled in dealing with such volumes of work. Otherwise there will not be any distinction between the working of a Manager and that of the non-managerial employees. Keeping normalcy in his temperament in dealing with the spate of work is very important which is essentially needed to work with efficiency and speed by a Manager, it requires strength of mind which is attained by devotion and practice.

The function of a Manager is variegated and not conventionalised. His mind has, therefore, to play in different ways in dealing with different nature of work and that too with maturity of thought. Maturity of thought is acquired through unruffled mind and practical experience. With cool brain and normal state of mind a successful Manager is required to sort out the intricacies of the problems. He will stumble at every stage if he becomes choleric in disposition in dealing with spate of work and thus he cannot win confidence in the higher management. A Manager cannot expect that he would be idling away in the office for insufficient work at his disposal but will be saddled with heaps of papers on his desk for disposal apart from doing other work of policy matters.

One important point is that keeping normalcy in dealing with spate of work, a Manager is essentially needed to be humourous and jovial which will exterminate his unsteady state of mind and he will find plain sailing in dealing with even the most complicated work. Success of a Manager is measured in terms of his steadiness and normalcy of mind at the time of dealing with the spate of work. But, at the same time his mind should not be diverted to other triffling matters when he is set to work of prime importance.

If a Manager is irked to find the volumes of work to be performed by him, disposal of the same will be procrastinated with the result that there will be continuous piling of work and it will go out of his capacity and control to deal with such voluminous work. He will then feel fish out of water and will be considered an inefficient Manager in the eyes of the higher management.

Under the circumstances, a Manager must be firm, steady and normal in dealing with spate of work if he is to be a successful Manager in the organisation.

Attaining Personal Development

14

In order to secure long-term career and organisational success a Manager has to learn things quickly/even if necessary from others. For professional development a Manager has to work on his weakest areas. He should build the habit of taking at least ten minutes time every day to review the key incidents of the last 24 hours. First he should look at what he did that worked and then at the same time look at what did not work. For reviewing all these, it is suggested that he should maintain a diary to jot down the day-to-day success he achieved and the affairs that he could not achieve. This will help him know where he stands, facilitating him to attain his personal development, because he will be able to assess both his success and weakness by his day's work. A Manager should know that personal professional development is critical to success in business, with personal development he will be able to motivate himself. A Manager should also read at least one book a month and create a library that can be referred to by him in future. He should take time to reflect on his development. His aim will be to learn something new every day. He has also to develop habit of reading papers and journals to keep him abreast of the up-to-date developments. A Manager has to spend his own money as an investment in his success. Generally, top performer allocates five per cent of his resources for improvement or his knowledge. With his personal development he can coach his staff members to solve their own problems with his support, rather than relying on him for solutions. Coaching is increasingly felt a necessity by top

Managers because it is one of the most effective ways of improving performance.

Prompt Disposal of Paper Work

15

Efficiency of a Manager is manifested through his quick disposal of papers/letters. Paper work is one of the important functions of a Manager. If a Manager is weak in disposal of papers/letters he cannot be considered a competent and successful Manager. There are of course reasons as to why a Manager takes dilatory action in dealing with the paper work which may be—either he is oscillating to take firm decision on matters of importance or he is devoid of conception to deal with matters. On account of dilatory process to deal with the paper work for the probable reasons as adduced above, there is deluge of huge papers on his desk and under this situation a Manager is totally confused what to do and it becomes an uphill task for him to overcome the impasse.

A Manager must always bear in mind that paper work is not the only part of his entire work but he has to make use of his valuable time to attend to other matters of importance also. Therefore, if a Manager has to devote his attention to face the spate of paper work only, he cannot do justice to the organisation as a Manager by his working. A Manager is no doubt a great expectation of the organisation. Paper work is not the only expectation of him by the higher management.

Now, the question arises how to deal with the spate of paper work, especially in respect of correspondence. Conception of ideas is a very important factor to deal with the correspondence. Through correspondence mental acumen of the Manager is exhibited as also the Company's image is upheld. For speedy disposal of paper work a Manager has to earmark those letters of policy matters to be dealt with by him only. As far as disposal of other letters is concerned, his PA/Assistant should be taken into confidence to draft out such letters.

By virtue of considerable period of his working in the organisation, a Manager must have thorough conception which will help him dispose of the letters of policy matters at the quickest possible time. Drafting knowledge of a Manager is also very important which will help quicken disposal of letters.

By following the above procedure to deal with the paper work, a Manager will get ample time to devote his attention in other matters and his competence and success in managerial capacity will be enhanced and he will be indispensable for the organisation he serves.

16

Working with Uncooperative and Difficult People

Working successfully with uncooperative and difficult individuals by maintaining improved performance and better working relationship is an essential management skill. In some organisations there may be a few officials/staff members who may not want that a Manager should enjoy the confidence of the highest echelon of the organisation by his most efficient working system and as such they may create certain problems or show their uncooperative and incalcitrant attitude to discredit the Manager in the discharge of his efficient services. In such situation, he has to be meticulous to adopt proven techniques and strategies to enable him to anticipate problem people, stop trouble from escalating and help awkward staff to become fully contributing members of the team. He should devise ways and means how to handle difficult people successfully by developing observation and communication skills, avoiding confrontation, working for cooperation and resolving conflict. It is the tendency of the difficult people that they stop the Manager achieving his goals. People who are difficult absorb his time and energy robing of his peace of mind so that he is rendered incapacitated to discharge his duties efficiently.

A Manager needs to understand what motivates difficult people and by whose instigation. Besides, before he can find a solution to prevent someone being difficult, he needs to define why the problem is happening. By his artifice and stratagem a

Manager has to bring the difficult people under his sway in a most peaceful way. A Manager who supports and encourages people to work together enthusiastically and shows appreciation for work well done, creates team spirit. He needs to be aware of the team's workload and what support individuals' need in order to do their job well. A Manager should communicate and let people participate in making decisions about their roles and the way they carry out their jobs. He should keep a watchful eye for signs of stress, irritation or depression in the people and he can gently give feedback on how they appear to them and how things are going. If the problem is personal, he should suggest different sources of external advice.

Showing bossism to the difficult people will not be wise on the part of the Manager, as the people are already in the know that he is managing the affairs of the organisation by holding the position of Manager. Sweet words from the Manager will soften the irritable attitude of the difficult people and work could be done with team spirit and here lies the success of a Manager. No job is mean in the eyes of a Manager. He should, therefore, praise the employees for any job done successfully by them. This will obviously create enthusiasm in the minds of the employees to bolster their activities in doing job in most effective way in future creating a sense of belonging to the organisation where they have been working. A Manager should realise that working closely with cooperative team members and ignoring a difficult colleague can move a situation forwards. Either the difficult team member will join in, or he will move away totally, in which case confrontation at a later date becomes inevitable. A Manager's primary aim is to gain the cooperation of difficult people. He should use good communication skills in order to obtain the best outcome from them.

Trustworthiness 17

A successful Manager must be trustworthy in his actions, behaviour and character. For a Manager it is of utmost necessity that he has to maintain interactions with the Management at the helm of affairs and other employees of the organisation and this interaction is based on trust. The working of a Manager without interaction and trust is void and he cannot be taken into confidence by the higher Management. It is very important for a Manager to work in the organisation with honour and dignity by creating trust. Now, the crux of the question is how to build trust. The factors for building trust are:

(a) The Manager has to build confidence by his sincerity and honesty of working,

(b) He must have unblemished character,

(c) He should give due respect to the dignified persons of the higher Management,

(d) He must have consistency between his words and deeds,

(e) He must prove his competence and attitude to service,

(f) He must be a person of integrity,

(g) He must create impression that he is a person of reliability,

If a Manager has lost confidence in the higher Management, he cannot enjoy the laurels of his position and hence he will always be a suspicious person. This is unbecoming of his managerial position in the organisation and his service career in such case will have a retrograde step. He will be considered unworthy of the position and the higher Management will think of getting rid of such Manager losing trust and confidence. Trustworthiness is a very important factor for a person working in higher position in any organisation.

A Manager has to know that following are the principal factors which cause distrust:

(a) Negative attitude,

(b) Lack of courtesy,

(c) Inconsistent and uncooperative behaviour,

(d) Lack of honesty and integrity,

(e) Selfishness

(f) Clandestine tendency to extract money from the company fraudulently.

Trust without integrity cannot be generated. A Manager must be a person of integrity if he has to maintain affinity and cordial relations with the higher Management by his trustworthiness. Therefore, a Manager has to think always that the trust he has created remains perpetual, as this will pave the way for further rise in his service career.

Providing Feedback to the Employees

18

The ability to use appraisal to develop and motivate employees is a core Management skill. It is the tendency of all the employees to know how their performance is viewed by their Manager. It is important on the part of the Manager to provide feedback continuously whether it is positive or negative. Proper feedback helps team members identify where they need to improve their skills, knowledge and attitudes. A Manager is likely not to be harsh while dealing with the employees. He should praise the employees for their achievements. A Manager should ensure that he is prepared for the arrival of new employees. Such new employees are likely to commit mistakes in the discharge of their duties in the new environment of the organisation. They are to be trained by the Manager as to how they are to be adaptable in the new situation so that they can feel easy to perform jobs assigned to them. This will help them perform jobs effectively. Under no circumstances, the Manager should utter harsh words to them for their failure to perform job effectively. This will help them build attachment with the Manager.

Team members must be committed to objectives if they are to carry out their tasks successfully. The team members who feel able to achieve an objective in their own way will take more responsibility for their achievement. A Manager should use appraisals to empower staff to gain their commitment to actions and to encourage them to use their own initiative. He should inspire staff members to think of different options for solving a problem as also allow them to learn from their own mistakes. A Manager should use appraisals to develop his team by discussing past successes and achievements so that they can be repeated and even surpassed. A Manager who encourages the team members to come up with ideas will get more from them. Ideas should never be criticised, since this will discourage people from voicing their suggestions. He should treat all his team members equally and fairly. Many appraisees may feel nervous and apprehensive at the start of their appraisal. The Manager has to help them overcome their anxieties by creating encouraging atmosphere. He should stress that the appraisal will have a positive result. If appraisees look confused the Manager should ensure that he is not using jargon so they do not understand.

A Manager should Listen to What the Employees Say

19

One of the prerequisites of a Manager is not to throttle the sentiments and/or views which the employees want to give vent to, rather he should encourage them to speak to him with their own reasoning which may not even be acceptable. This will help the Manager to correct their wrong conceptions and the employees will feel enthused to know the unknown. In this way, the employees will find opportunity to develop their knowledge of working.

While listening to the employees the Manager has to see that –

(a) He should never speak more than listening,

(b) He should not interrupt when the employees are continuing to speak,

(c) He should give a patient hearing to the employees without being absent-minded,

(d) He should be a good listener in order to inspire the employees to express their views, as listening shows caring attitude of the Manager and the employees will feel more motivated,

(e) While listening he should avoid distractions,

(f) When the employees are speaking on a particular topic, the Manager should not change the subject of discussions,

(g) While listening he should show due respect and understanding,

(h) While the employees are speaking on a particular topic, they should be made to feel by the Manager that he is showing empathy,

(i) While listening the Manager should have eye contact with the employees.

By adhering to the above strategems of listening to the employees by the Manager, this is also another way of creating situations by which the employees will feel motivated in their working and the success of a Manager will be manifested when the employees are motivated. What is needed most is that a Manager must have to draw asunder the barriers to effective listening. Enkindling enthusiasm in the minds of the employees is a part of function of a successful Manager and the creation of enthusiasm is the result of effective listening by the Manager. Enthusiasm inspires confidence and builds royalty to the Manager by the employees.

It is, therefore, incumbent on the part of the Manager to realise how effective it is to have a patient hearing to what the employees want to express. In this connection, the Manager should also remember that he should not go on continuing to listen to the employees most of the time at the cost of his other work, for which he has to allot time for the employees.

Maintaining Public Relations by a Manager

20

Maintaining public relations by a Manager comprises his practical skills and strategies designed to enhance the reputation of an organisation. Improving staff communication and public/customer care, dealing with crises and organising events and campaigns are key public relations skills. Managing public relations guides him to success in his working. This is also a valuable guide to the skills a Manager needs for an essential business discipline. Public relation is a powerful tool that can make a vital contribution to the organisational success. Public relation is an effective communication between an organisation and the public. True purpose of public relation is to create a well-deserved reputation of an organisation and it is the Manager who has to maintain public relation by his practical skills and strategies. Maintaining public relations has the following advantages:

(a) To build stronger and more lasting relationship with the clients,

(b) To increase the public's awareness of the organisation,

(c) To promote a new range of products more widely.

Good communication enables a Manager to build lasting relationships with the people averting misunderstanding that leads to ill-will. Poor communication leaves customers feelings ignored and disinclined to do business with the organisation. A Manager has to assess the effectiveness of all his communication methods, such as letters, e-mail, face-to-face talks and publicity materials. He has also to ensure that the people will feel easy to communicate with him. When any message by way of a letter is received, it should be replied promptly. A Manager has to realise that while talking to the people either in his office or in their office, he should express his pleasing attitude with smiles and open heartedness. This will create a good impression in the minds of the people, solidifying the public relations between them and the organisation. While talking to the people there should be eye contact which indicates closeness of mind between them and the Manager. A Manager has also to remember that the way of maintaining public relations is based on the organisation's corporate strategy. Measuring effectiveness is an important element of strategic public relations. The aim of measuring is to assess whether or not objectives have been achieved.

Not to Indulge in Loose Talks and Avoiding Criticism Aimed at the Employees

21

Sentiments of human beings are very much perceptible by sense. String of heart is very soft and touchy. It is extremely susceptible even at the slightest friction. Such being the circumstances, employees are to be treated with extreme caution and care. Since they have sense of respectability—no matter whether they may work in humble position, a Manager has to see that while dealing with them, their sentiments are not hurt by uttering loose talks, otherwise, their minds will be tormented and it will affect the working of the organisation on account of resorting to go-slow tactic by the employees. If the Manager has to educate the employees to rectify their follies in working, they are to be educated not by shouting and showing red eyes but by words spiced with tenderness, love and affection. This in effect will motivate them and they will take extreme caution and care not to commit the same mistakes in their working in future. They will also hold the Manager with respectability. Talking in tender mindedness with the employees by the Manager does not in any way exhibit his weakness but highness of his mind. Therefore, a Manager should never indulge in loose talks with the employees. He should maintain gravity and control his tongue which will gravitate the employees towards him.

As far as the word 'criticism' is concerned, it is of two types—one is to criticise the person and the other is to criticise the working of the person. Criticism has also another distinguishing feature, i.e. positive criticism and negative criticism. It is always desirable that if one has to criticise the working of the person it should be constructive and not negative. Otherwise, he will be down-hearted and will lose inspiration to work with zeal and enthusiasm. It has also to be taken care of that while criticising self-esteem of the person is not hurt.

When the definition of criticism is as such that no employee should be criticised personally by the Manager, but his working, the Manager has to see that while indulging in positive criticism of the working of the employees it must have stimulating effect. Following are the ways as to how to criticise the working of the employees for the purpose of heightening motivation.

(a) In the criticism there should be full of suggestions for improving the working of the employees,

(b) While criticising, opportunity has to be given to explain the position of the employees,

(c) Criticism should centre round the benefits the employees have to derive by correcting their mistakes,

(d) Criticism should be made privately and not in presence of other employees,

(e) In the criticism there should not be words of intimidation,

(f) Criticism should be made with helping attitude,

(g) Criticism should not be ambiguous so as to avoid resentment in the minds of the employees,

(h) While criticising, the Manager is to be cool minded and firm.

Criticising the working of the employees in positive and constructive ways is very necessary in order to ensure mistake-free working. This will help the employees to be more cautious in their working in future. Hence, criticism made by the Manager should be taken by the employees in right perspective and also they should accept the same as benediction. Managers have to ensure that on no occasion they should criticise the employees personally but their performance. They should also offer solutions in their criticism.

Balancing Work and Life of a Manager

22

On account of pressure of work Managers fall into the trap of working long hours in the office almost everyday neglecting relationships, self-development, leisure pursuits and personal happiness. Balancing work and life will help him understand what success means to him. A Manager has to realise that time is his most valuable resource. His ability to save time or waste time determines how well he balances his work and life. As he begins to achieve a better balance in his work and life, he will discover new levels of creativity, fulfilment and happiness. People often work hard to gain "success" without knowing what success really means. A Manager may climb a career ladder, but is he fulfilled by his work? Does he has a good home life? Success comes from leading a fulfilled and balanced life. A Manager should, therefore, try to balance his work and life more effectively. He enjoys his job when he leaves the office on time so that he can spend time with his family. Success is an attitude and not a financial gain. In fact, many rich, famous and accomplished people have material success but do not actually feel truly successful. Success is not just found in outer things, but is located within oneself. One should cultivate success as a state of mind. It is important to have a positive, proactive attitude so that a Manager can lead his life with purpose and vision. It is found that family life of a Manager is being damaged by his constant striving for financial gain. But by involving his family in developing a new vision, he is able to lead his life with renewed purpose.

While working in office a Manager should ask questions to himself which are as follows:

(a) Do I work longer hours than I need to?

(b) Am I achieving something important or am I just keeping myself busy?

(c) Do I feel guilty if I am the first person to leave the office?

(d) How could I prioritize my time more effectively?

If a Manager is always busy when he is under pressure of work, he should allot his timings by deciding the following:

(a) First of all, he has to recognize that he is overloaded with urgent tasks,

(b) He should look at the tasks that are critical and must be done,

(c) He should decide which tasks can be put on hold or delegated,

(d) He should concentrate on the critical tasks and work more effectively.

Eschewing the Habit of Back-Biting

23

A Manager must be clean-minded possessing moral integrity. He should not blow hot and cold in the same breath. A Manager ought to know that drawing respects from others cannot be purchased. He may nurture the idea that by virtue of his position in the organisation employees would show their respects towards him. But, it is not a correct conception of a Manager. True respect comes from the core of heart. Showing outward respect is artificial. If a Manager is a dubious and a double standard person and also in the habit of back-biting/he as a Manager is not a sophisticated person in the eyes of the employees and the higher management too. Back-biting, if it is resorted to by a Manager, cannot pay him anything rather his position will be slandered, with such habit he will not be treated as a reliable person and the employees cannot expect of such Manager to do anything good for them, with back-biting tendency of a Manager even the position of an honest, sincere and hard working employee may be jeopardised in the eyes of the higher Management if such employee happens to be in sordid relation with the Manager for any unforeseen circumstances and even the services of such employee may be at stake for no fault of him.

Under any circumstances, no Manager should resort to the habit of back-biting which is injurious not only for him but also for the organisation and the employees.

Back-biting is considered as perversion of a person and no Manager with such habit can think of winning confidence in the higher Management and working in any organisation for a longer period of time. The employees working under him will heave a sigh of relief if such a Manager quits the organisation at the soonest.

The persons who have innate desire to work as Managers by acquiring required qualifications and also who are already working in managerial capacity, must not entertain any idea of becoming double standard persons with tendency of back-biting in the interest of their working as successful Managers. Persons practising the habit of back-biting are abominable and hypocritical. They cannot develop unblemished character. Such persons are unfit to shoulder higher responsibilities in the office in the capacity of Manager, because they are derelict of managerial quality with such inclination of back-biting.

Giving Guidance and Coaching to Staff Members

24

As a Manager it is his job to ignite the team spirit. He has to see how best a team will work together. When he is creating a team culture, he should focus on vision, values, relationships and work-life balance. A Manager should make it known to the team members that they do not require to give their everything for the job they perform at the cost of their home lives. It is not the interest of the Manager that team members are overloaded with work. If they are heavily burdened with work teamwork deteriorates, relationships suffer and the team spirit dries up. The Manager should realize that overworking blunts performance and long hours of working on regular basis do not necessarily increase productivity. The Manager has to monitor the health of his team members and keep eyeing on their energy. If the team members are driven to exhaustion, they will not be able to produce the desired results and the Manager will lose their loyalty that they bestow to him.

For a team to work well, each and every team member must work to his optimum personal effectiveness. The Manager has to coach his staff to have a better work-life balance. He should teach others what he wants to practise himself. Right balance between work and life varies from people to people. The Manager should build rapport, listen, understand and then create a programme to suit individual needs. While it is the interest of the Manager that his team members have healthy home lives, business of the organisation does sometimes involve the team members in unpredictable change, busy seasons, unforeseen meetings, weekend conferences etc. In such situation, the team members have not to leave the office on time and that they should not groan as such situations are not regular in their work activities. They should bear in mind that the organisation where they work is their bread earner and that they are prepared always to adapt themselves in such situations in the interest of prosperity of the organisation. When the staff members have worked long hours to meet a difficult deadline on a project, the Manager should thank them for their extra efforts and entertain them with light refreshments. This will generate in them the sense of belonging to the organisation.

Attitude of a Manager

25

Positive attitude of a Manager contributes to success. It applies to every sphere of life including one's personal and professional life. A Manager cannot be a successful Manager without having positive attitude. Foundation of success depends upon positive attitude. A person with positive attitude is like a fruit of all seasons. The following are the benefits of positive attitude:

(a) Fosters team work in an organisation,

(b) Improves quality of work,

(c) Fosters better relationships with the higher Management/employees and the customers,

(d) Makes for congenial atmosphere,

(e) Generates loyalty in the minds of the employees,

(f) Helps solve problems.

Therefore, a Manager with positive attitude can have the advantages of all the above which will lead to his success in the field of his profession.

In this connection, it will be appropriate to mention as to how to develop positive attitude, if a Manager is devoid of the same. The ways are:

(a) Be aware of the principles that build a positive attitude,

(b) Desire to be positive,

(c) Cultivate discipline and dedication.

The Manager should always bear in mind that negative attitude breeds bitterness and resentment in the minds of the higher management and the employees. Also a Manager with negative attitude is in the habit of finding faults with every employee and every situation which will negate systematic working in the office. Therefore, a Manager must abjure negative attitude in the interest of attaining success in the field of his profession.

How to Deal with Stress by a Manager

26

It is an admitted fact that stress is an increasingly a common feature of human beings in modern living. It saps working capability. A Manager has to realize that on account of having stress his work-life balance is under threat. He is required to be free from stress as he is to remain healthy and without being disturbed for the purpose of shouldering higher responsibilities in the discharge of his duties in office. Stress is the result of anxiety. A Manager has to identify the cause of his anxiety. He should never be anxious to solve any problem. He should take things easy and remain calm and quite when he is faced with problem, when he is feeling stressed he should make fun with others, in order to do away with stress he should also take the following steps:

(a) He should make it a point of choosing to think positive thoughts,

(b) He should do regular 'pranayam' (breathing exercise) to help cleanse his body and remain free from disease,

(c) He should make sure that he keeps his body properly nourished by taking nourishing food such as plenty of fruit and vegetables during the day so that he has a rich source of vitamins and minerals. He should also drink at least two litres of water per day in winter and three litres per day in summer.

(d) He should avail of the lunch time in the office strictly so that he can have his lunch on time everyday,

(e) He should sleep well. If, however, he is having problem of sleeping he should eat a banana an hour before bedtime,

(f) He should commit to spending time with the people he loves,

(g) He should choose social events he wants to attend,

(h) He should consider work more enjoyable rather than viewing it as an unenjoyable task.

Relaxation is very important for a good work-life balance. A Manager has to realize which ways of relaxation will be suitable for him. Some people like to practise meditation, read quietly or have long hot baths. Others prefer playing sports, going to the cinema or enjoying meal with friends. A Manager should relax regularly in order to rejuvenate his health, enjoy his life and improve performance of his work.

What should be the Relation a Manager has to Maintain with the Subordinate Staff Members

27

Employees are no doubt inseparable members in an organisation. Although a Manager is one of the pillars of an organisation, the employees are the supporting pillars. Hence, the employees are to be given due weightage and cognisance of performance of their duties, it is not possible on the part of a Manager himself to do the entire job alone of his subordinates, although he is in the know of the job performed by them. A Manager has to depend upon the employees in the discharge of duties. Therefore, in order to run a company smoothly and efficiently, there must be complete cohesion and cooperation among the Manager and the subordinate staff members. Success of a Manager depends upon the cooperative attitude with the employees. Hence, in order to become a successful Manager, it is absolutely necessary that his relations and attitude with his subordinates will be:

(a) A Manager should treat the employees in such a way that they are not made to feel that they have no standing and status in the organisation. He should also create such a situation that the employees develop a sense of belonging to the company they serve and that they are always at the beck and call of the Manager,

(b) Human mind is very much touchy and sensitive. Therefore, a Manager should not injure the sentiment of the employees by talking with them in irrational way. By sweet words from the Manager, the minds of the employees are softened and work is performed in a very peaceful atmosphere,

(c) A Manager has never to indulge in resorting to discriminatory attitude. He should treat all the employees with equal eyes irrespective of the position they hold. This will create homogeneity in the minds of the employees,

(d) He should have soft corner in his mind to understand the genuine difficulties of the employees and find his way to help the employees financially at times when they are badly in need of money arising out of their unforeseen and emergent financial commitments. This will help them to be worry-free and the work of the company will not meet with rebuff,

(e) Previously, the concept of employment was master and servant relations. But, now this concept has changed altogether as employee-employer relations. Therefore, although a Manager is a management staff, yet his relations with the subordinates will be very sweet and cordial in view of the changed situation in modern-day employment. This means that there should be close affinity between the Manager and the subordinate employees,

(f) Although close and sweet relations should persist between the Manager and the subordinate staff members, yet a Manager should not allow laxity while dealing with the erring employees, else there will be slackening in the maintenance of administration, which will be disastrous for the organisation.

In order, therefore, to attain success and popularity, a Manager has to deal with the employees by the above principles, which is very important for all the Managers in the modern-day employment scenario.

Tasks before a Manager to Streamline the Working of an Organisation

28

An organisation sinks due to defective policy of the higher Management creating financial debilitation and lawlessness in the working of the employees, in such situations a Manager has a greater role to play to set right the overall working of the sinking organisation. First of all, the Manager has to study the affairs of the dying organisation. He then has to use the most up-to-date and proven methods to help everyone think about performance. He can achieve success by helping others to improve and work towards common goals. The Manager has to realize that some employees will pose problems to him which may be difficult to overcome. Understanding why people are difficult helps him anticipate their behaviour and take action to prevent problems and reduce conflict. The employees are to be educated that by adopting the tactic of lawlessness in their working they will not gain anything rather their future will be doomed. This sense of awareness in their minds is to be enlivened. By his leadership quality the Manager will be able to win the confidence of the obstinate and nagging employees and bring them under his complete control. The Manager will need an effective appraisal system that can incorporate clear and comprehensive personal development plans to enable everyone to understand what success means to them. In the process of streamlining and rejuvenating the organisational work by the employees, the Manager will of course find himself in situations that no one has faced before. To be successful in his endeavour he has to maintain both his personal skills and knowledge and use the latest techniques to motivate and encourage the employees to accept his leadership and ideas.

While the higher Management will start observing the perceptible change in the working of the employees which has been made possible by the skill and competence of the Manager, the actions of the Manager will be given complete recognition by them and in turn the Manager will have upper hand with the higher Management. This will help him convince the Management to change their erroneous policy which is detrimental to the interest of the organisation. By virtue of the skill/competence and experience of the Manager the higher Management will amend their policy for the better and the working of the organisation will be back to normalcy. This is of course an arduous task on the part of the Manager but he will be crowned with success to revitalise the organisation by his unstinted and spirited efforts.

Intelligence

29

Every Manager must have intelligence quotient (I.Q.). In his capacity as Manager since he may have to take many actions on the spot instantaneously he must be in the know that every action has reaction and in multiple cases such reactions may be detrimental to the interest of the organisation which he must avoid. But how? This will be possible when he has the intellectual capability and sharpness of mind to surmise what would likely to take place arising out of such actions taken by him. Here lies his success as a Manager. A Manager has obviously to deal with the intricacies of matters which require tactful handling in the interest of the organisation. Such tactful handling of matters requires his intelligence. A person without intelligence can never think of becoming a Manager, because he will be a bankrupt of managerial qualities in absence of the same.

Intelligence of a Manager helps overcome many problems which he faces during the course of his working. Moreso, by virtue of his intelligent decisions in matters of insurmountable problems facing any organisation, he paves the way to come in the limelight as a magnetic force in the eyes of the higher Management and his prospect in the organisation is widened. Needless to emphasise, intelligence is an indispensable qualification for a Manager. By virtue of his intelligence he will have quick grasping capacity of things which is one of the plus points to act as Manager. In order to work tactfully a Manager has to study the psychology and sentiments of the employees and this becomes possible when he has the analytical capacity and the intelligence of the Manager plays a great role in this respect.

It is evident how intelligence of a Manager is important in the performance of his duties. Such a Manager with intelligence quotient can never become unsuccessful.

This chapter will be incomplete if it is not discussed how intelligence of a person could be developed. It is of course an admitted fact that intelligence of a person has its own originality. But still then it could be developed further by the following methods which are analysed seriatim.

(a) Desire of a person to come to a definite conclusion after analysing the facts and circumstances of matters,

(b) Mixing up with different strata of people to know about their views of variegated nature,

(c) Mixing up with the galaxy of intellectuals to know about their perception of things,

(d) By way of gleaning practical experience,

(e) Propensity to know the unknown,

(f) Contemplation on any matter seriously to know its bright/dark side.

If all these are practised there will be broadening of mental faculties thereby developing intelligence of a person.

Ability to Handle Situations

30

Ability to handle situations effectively under crying circumstances is a vital element of becoming a successful Manager. During the course of working a Manager cannot expect that he will have plain sailing throughout in the discharge of his duties. Awkward situation is bound to emanate and he has to remain firm and stubborn to confront with such situation. By identifying the areas of his performance that he needs to improve he has to change his thoughts, assumptions and emotions so that he can improve the results. In most of the cases, emotional intelligence of a Manager plays a very important role. Emotional intelligence is that how well he manages himself and his working relationships with others. A Manager has, therefore, to increase his effectiveness by developing his emotional intelligence skills. Intelligence Quotient (I.Q.) or technical competence is also necessary by a Manager to handle situation but in terms of its percentage it is only 15%, as the research shows. There are two aspects of emotional intelligence that determine performance as a Manager. The first is his ability to handle situations in an effective manner and the second is his ability to be sensitive in the knowing of the performance of others.

Rigid attitude will not always help handling situations effectively by a Manager. He has to be flexible in his approach by adapting to match the different types of situation. It is necessary to choose the right methods to obtain outstanding results. If a Manager perceives that it is very hard to deal with a situation having negative points and is not negotiable which may frustrate him, he has to decide which aspect of his approach is the easiest to change. He should feel motivated and not frustrated under any circumstances. He should have the ability to develop flexibility to handle situation at work by changing aspects of his feelings, beliefs and thoughts.

It is the aim of the Manager to see that his working performance is maximised even in stressful situations. When he has to deliver something important but cannot because of other commitments, he is likely to be stressed and his work will suffer. In order to cope with stressful situations he can change his perception of the situation until it becomes a positive challenge or he can change his emotional state to deal with it better.

Keeping Healthy Mind and Sound Health

31

The duties of a Manager are as such that he has to deal with matters of importance and intricacies with cool brain and mind. A Manager possessing sound health is a person of activity, which is needed most to execute work with efficiency. Ill health devours his working capacity. Unless a Manager is a person of activity he cannot do justice to the work entrusted to him. He has not only to do office work but also to keep himself preoccupied with outside work such as contacting with the officials—both government and non-government—attending court cases etc. For this purpose, he has to be invigorated and activated with healthy mind and sound health.

Efficiency of a Manager could be maintained when he would keep himself busy in doing jobs entrusted to him by taking care of maintaining sound health and keeping healthy mind. On the other hand, he will prove himself inefficient when he will be failing sick sporadically and will continue to remain absent from attending office time and again which will affect his working very much. Therefore, in order to keep healthy mind and sound health, it is absolutely necessary that he has to go for excursion tours at least once in every year. This will freshen his mind and body and he will feel enthusiasm to work with strength, vigour, zeal and freshness after return from such tours. The purpose of arranging such tours is to revitalise the working spirit of the Manager which will be of great advantage for the organisation too.

Apart from this, Managers are to be made members of Lions club or any other clubs which are the concentration of galaxy of intellectuals. Mingling with the personalities attending to such clubs after office hours will be very much conducive for the Managers to lessen their clumsiness and fatigue after working in the office with tension. Mental make-up of the Managers will also be developed by mixing up with such personalities in the club and also it will help develop the business relations with different organisations which in turn will benefit the organisation in many ways. Becoming members of such clubs is, therefore, absolutely necessary for the persons working in managerial capacity to preserve their efficiency of working by way of keeping healthy mind and sound health and also upkeep of business relations. This is also one of the factors as to how a Manager could be successful in the discharge of his duties and he will feel oneness to the organisation, which the higher Management expects from a Manager.

Making Self-Assessment by a Manager

32

Primarily a Manager has no doubt to think deeply about his criteria for success in his working. He has to analyse whether his work has enriched the whole of his life or his family life is a shift from the work or his work only has justified fulfilment in his life. A Manager has to know that he should also take keen interest in outside work. In order to enjoy a healthy balanced work-life, he should be careful to assess that such balance is required to be kept up at any cost for becoming efficient in his working in office. He should be in the know that his family life will be neglected and damaging totally if he patronizes his work only. If he does not take care of his children in the midst of pressure of work, there will be every possibility that his children will be denied opportunities to come up in life, which will not bring peace of mind to him. Ultimately, the Manager is to be superannuated from service on reaching certain age but when sons in particular are well placed in life on account of taking proper care of them in the midst of his working, they will be his personal assets when he will be leading a life of recluse after his retirement from service. Hence, self-assessment on the part of a Manager is very important in his practical life.

A Manager has to think always about the critical roles he has to play in his life. He should consider what he wants to achieve in life in his roles. Perception of a Manager is very important when he thinks of his life as a whole—his work, family, friends, personal development and finally doing good for the community where he lives. He should realize that success is about all aspects of his life and not just doing work in office. He should also perceive that if he wants to further his academic and professional studios in the course of his working, he can do so. Such desire of furthering studies depends upon quenching his thirst for enhancement of qualifications if he is short of the same.

In order to achieve cohesion between work and life the Manager will need to review his progress in this direction constantly. Self-assessment helps fulfilment in life. A Manager should plan action by his sensitivity to emotions, assessment of his priorities, beliefs, perceptions and choices. A Manager can enjoy greater happiness in life by improving his emotional intelligence. Emotional intelligence is his ability to manage his feelings and thoughts. Emotional intelligence enhances his power of decision-making and of thinking more clearly and taking matured decision. He should be aware of that his feelings are a gateway to creativity, intuition and inspiration. Self-assessment will help him evaluate his real priorities and focus his attention on them which will bring him success in life. He can think what is essential to him. By his self-assessment he can also decide whether it is necessary for him to do a work personally or if it is possible to delegate to others providing positive or negative results.

Contributing Factors which Determine the Effectiveness of a Manager

33

When a Manager wants to be successful in his duties and functions doing justice to the organisation in his capacity as Manager, there must be contributing factors which would make him effective. An effective Manager is an asset of the organisation and is inalienable from the higher Management. Such an effective Manager can enjoy the full confidence of the highest echelon of the Management. Here lies his greatest satisfaction and the co-officers and the employees will hold him in high esteem. The following are the contributing factors which determine the effectiveness of a Manager:

(a) Business protocol

A Manager must have the sense of business protocol. Business protocol generates relationship, drives cooperation and fuels communication.

(b) Effective listening

Effective listening by a Manager pleases employees and other people. This demonstrates his open mind, which is the key to communication. The essentials of effective listening are to list—

- Without interruption
- Without switching of
- With intent for understanding

- Avoiding distractions
- Showing respect and understanding
- Having eye contact with employees.

(c) Attitude

It is a way a Manager has to communicate his mood to others. Positive attitude is a mindset without which nothing worthwhile can be achieved. Positive attitude breeds positive results.

(d) Motivation

An effective Manager should encourage and inspire people to motivate themselves.

(e) Decision making

An effective Manager has to identify the real causes of any problem before arriving at a decision. He has also to think of far-reaching consequences before arriving at a final decision.

(f) Relationship

An effective Manager must take special care to maintain relationship with the co-officers and the subordinates. In dealing with the subordinates, the important steps to be taken by the effective Manager are:

- Knowing the subordinates
- Lending ears to listen
- Showing patience
- Remaining firm but not angry.

How does a Manager Think of Developing a Dynamic Career?

34

A Manager reaches zenith of his success and attains fulfilment in working life on his past experience. He cannot think of his dynamic career immediately after he starts working as a Manager. Pacing problems and tribulations during the course of his working for certain period of years are the criteria to make him dynamic with the result that he becomes a seasoned Manager attaining perfection in his working. Handling crises and change are the key aspects of developing dynamic career of a Manager. He becomes straightforward in his thinking and actions by his dynamism. Every ambitious Manager has to think that his working is not a bed of roses. He will think that it is his sport to handle knotty problems and work out solutions to such problems successfully. By his self-assessment he will be able to evaluate himself where he stands and makes himself definite which one is correct and wrong.

No Manager achieves success and happiness at work by chance. He has to attain the same by virtue of his working hard and facing difficult situations as well as handling odds and ends of working life. Attaining dynamic career is a long journey. It is not achieved over night. Successful career paths of a Manager have good planning and a sense of direction. After attaining successful career a Manager is not to think that it is all that he has attained. He will be methodical at every stage of his working as a successful and dynamic Manager and then only he will feel at ease and comfortable at work without vacillation. By virtue of gleaning experience a Manager will be fully equipped to anticipate situations which are going to happen and accordingly he can prepare himself to make sensible and realistic plans to act upon them. This will create more confidence in himself.

When the Manager will be able to shape his career by his experience of working, he will feel challenged, stimulated and enchanted at work. Also when his career goals are achieved, he will feel a great sense of satisfaction. When a Manager attains dynamic career he is gifted with three aspects of things—attention, analysis and evaluation. These three requisite things are the essence of a competent Manager. First, he can pay more attention to events that have taken place. Second, he can analyze the causes and effects of any matter. Third, he can evaluate the consequences of any decision that he has taken.

Style of Functioning of a Manager

35

Style of functioning of a Manager plays a very important role to consolidate his position in the organisation where he works. He should work in such a manner that it does not irk the employees thereby generating discontent in their minds out of the discourteous way of his working. Keeping the employees happy by his style of working should be the motto of a Manager. A Manager will be alienated from the employees when his style of working is not to the liking of the employees. In such case he will be a misfit in the organisation. His working in the capacity of Manager will meet with rebuff and he will be the most unpopular Manager for his peculiar and strange way of working. Under the circumstances, is it worthwhile on the part of a Manager to pervert his normal style of working? The answer must be in the negative. Style of working of a Manager must be methodical befitting to the organisational set-up. A Manager will work with honour and dignity in the organisation only when his style of working will be on the following basis:

(a) A Manager has to keep the General Manager/President/Managing Direct or Chairman of the organisation abreast of the functioning of his section/department at regular intervals,

(b) Taking note of the points which the General Manager/President/Managing Director/Chairman directs for implementation and informing him/them of the progress achieved in this direction,

(c) Arranging meetings with the Section Incharges from time to time to know about their problems, if any, for redressal,

(d) To give suggestions in writing for efficient running of the organisation to the General Manager/President with copy to Managing Director/Chairman,

(e) To obtain progress report of the working of the employees every fortnight from the Section Incharges,

(f) To maintain good liaison with the outsiders coming to the organisation for business talks,

(g) To think of the development/progress of the organisation bearing in mind that it is his own organisation,

(h) To deal with the matters in the best interest of the organisation depending upon the exigency of circumstances,

(i) To take rational view in dealing with the employees,

(j) Finally, his style of working will be in conformity with the system of working prevailing in the organisation.

When the Manager will be able to mould his style of working in the above fashions he will be regarded as the most successful Manager of the organisation and will be considered an asset in the eyes of the higher Management.

36

Plan to Develop Career as a Successful Executive other than the Position of Manager

When undertaking journey without earmarking a destination is a miscalculation and has no meaning, haphazard way of planning to attain successful career is a distant dream. A Manager has, therefore, to plan in a constructive and systematic way to attain success in his career. He has to think that it is not all that his dream has come to reality by becoming a Manager. Being clear about how to achieve goals, a Manager will maximise his chances of success, if he is at all career-minded. He must always look ahead to work in exalted position beyond what he is now working in the capacity of Manager even when he is happy at work, working as Manager is not the end of a career-minded Manager. Determination must be there to ascend the ladder of much higher position. Continuing to cling to the position of Manager for all the years without mobility in official position will ultimately bring monotony in his working and he will lose flavour in the discharge of his duties as a Manager.

When he perceives that the chance of his getting promotion beyond his official position of Manager in the present organisation is bleak, he should look for a better position in other organisation of repute where he can think of his rosy future by virtue of his vast experience of working. But, before moving to such organisation, he must take stock of its financial soundness and the character of the higher Management with whom he has to work maintaining close liaison. A Manager should of course never think of moving from one organisation to another like a shuttlecock every now and then which will exhibit his unstable mind to work in one organisation for a longer period. This will not speak high of him.

The results he achieves depend upon the choices and decisions that he makes. He is responsible for the choices that he makes. A career Manager has a proactive approach to life. Some people have an early career idea that sustains them for years. They gain in determination. There are other Managers who are vague about what they want to achieve. They may benefit in certain cases from being flexible over their career options but may not progress very fast. The best way is to work to a structured plan to give them a sense of direction and prevent drift in career development. A Manager must have the instinct of making self-analysis and should learn about himself by evaluating his past experience. He should know what he wants to achieve and by which time-frame.

A Manager as an Administrator

37

Competence of a Manager is adjudged by his way of administering the affairs in the best interest of the organisation. A Manager who is vacillant in his actions stumbles in his working at every step and in such case he is an utter failure to discharge his responsibilities. What is needed is that a Manager must be a person of strong will force and has controlling capacity. Employees will have the confidence in the actions taken by a Manager when the same are in the best interest of the organisation and the employees as a whole. A Manager must be a person having mental acumen and personality and then only he will be in a position to discharge his duties as an administrator in true sense of the term in the capacity of his designated post of Manager. His way of administration will be as such that he must be bold enough to deal with any knotty problems during the course of his working. His administration must be acclaimed with commendation in the eyes of others. He must have the capacity to sort out even the invincible problems by applying his intellectual capability.

For the purpose of maintaining his administration in the best interest of the organisation, he must have argues eyes over what is happening all around his office so that his administration does not end in fiasco. Higher Management has inviolable faith in the administration of the Manager when he justifies his capability by his foresightedness and experience. Maintenance of administration is vital for a Manager on which depends trouble-free running of the organisation. Hence, the

Manager's responsibility in his performance as an Administrator is a stupendous task.

It is an admitted fact that administrative acumen is wanting in many organisations. Capable Managers with administrative acumen are the panacea for the organisations facing closure on account of being sick, so that such organisations are restored for economic resuscitation. Competent Managers working in organisations must be fully devoted so that they prove themselves assets by virtue of their administrative skills. Managers working in the organisations must be fully trained up so as to enable them to push the organisations to ascend to the position of all-round viability by dint of their administrative skill and competence.

Ensuring Discipline and Dress of a Manager

38

Instances are plenty that many talented persons have not been crowned with success in their lives. They have not tried to realize that their failures to attain success were on account of their leading lives recklessly and in indisciplined way. Haphazard way of working is not discipline. Discipline is something different. Discipline is a regulated and systematic way of doing things. Peace and happiness of a person comes when he is disciplined. Practice of discipline helps a person reach the desired goal. Discipline is the yardstick for progress of human beings. Human life is now very much complex and hence easy and peaceful life is conspicuous by its absence in most of the cases. Disciplined way of working is the only answer to bringing peace, happiness and regulated life. Hence, discipline is very important for every human life.

Having discussed the importance of discipline in the foregoing, it is absolutely necessary that a Manager is also required to be disciplined. Otherwise, system of his working will be in complete disarray. In order to become a successful Manager he has to enforce discipline. Strong administration in an organisation is the result of the enforcement of discipline. In absence of maintenance of discipline by a Manager, employees become obstinate, reckless and uncontrolable which is pernicious for the organisation. Also when discipline is impaired, lawlessness prevails everywhere and the organisation crumbles into economic degeneration and ultimately it is threatened with closure. Maintenance of discipline brings prosperity to an organisation. Disciplined way of working is the answer to attaining efficiency by a Manager and when he is efficient it is his responsibility to see that discipline is upheld. With a view to attaining this, he himself should be a man of discipline and then only he can enforce discipline in the organisation.

Costume of a Manager

There should be pink of perfection in the dress of a Manager he puts on. Office decorum is very important. Wearing decent dress by a Manager is a part of maintaining office decorum. Office of the Manager is prestigeous and hence in order to maintain prestige of his office, he should also put on decent costume. Moreso, by wearing dress of good taste a Manager looks elegant and a person of personality which speaks well of him in the eyes of the higher Management. Smartness of a Manager is an important factor for his efficient working and he looks smart when he wears good dress. Wearing-quality dress he can also leave a good impression in the minds of the high officials of other organisation when he calls on them for any official purpose. So, wearing graceful dress by a Manager has tremendous impact in the business organisation.

A Manager has to Assess Situations

39

Human beings are living in different stages of lives and that they have to adapt themselves in the midst of changing situations. A Manager has to analyse his present situation/ realize in which direction he is moving and/or progressing and what lies ahead of him. Making assessment of the same is the key so as to enable him to mould his career successfully. Every Manager can reap the harvest by checking the progress for his better career. Even when he feels that everything is progressing well, he can bc satisfied that his career path is more or less free from constraints and that he will be able to maintain steady progress in his life-time remaining in exalted position of service. He has to maintain three aspects without fail. First, he has to pay more attention to events which are changing. Second, he has to study closely what benefits have been accrued by him out of his experience he has gleaned and third, he has to evaluate the results of the decisions/actions taken by him. There is absolute need for the Manager out of his assessment of the present situation that he should—

(a) Face crisis,

(b) Make crucial decisions,

(c) Recover from difficult situation,

(d) Improve future prospects,

(e) End a period of drift,

(f) Take more control over all areas of life, and

(g) Consider how his present behaviour could influence his future.

A Manager has to think about his goals envisaging where he wants to get to and how he intends to get there. A Manager should make sure that he has to choose the way of working that feels most comfortable to him. When he feels that his career became most successful in the past and there is every reason that he feels happy now, it will be an indication of the situation that will add to his strength and energy to work more efficiently and also after he gets the patronage, inspiration and commendation from the higher Management. If the Manager perceives that the higher Management is not expressing enthusiasm and is disliking his working because of their biasness he will obviously feel fish out of water with the result that his efficient working will be eroded and his continuance in the organisation will be ephemeral. In such situation, his only option will be to see his way to make change of his present employment in the organisation. The concerned Manager is to know that for such officials the higher Management adopts pressure tactic to get rid of them. A Manager has to understand that after getting himself fixed up in a new organisation it takes six months in any new position to feel really confident about it.

How to Explore Possibilities of Source of Employment by a Manager?

40

When advertisement through newspaper is made for recruitment of Managers and for similar other posts, heaps of applications are received by the organisation for filling up the vacancies. For such method of filling up vacancies it takes considerable time to recruit hands after sorting out the applications. In order to avoid delay in recruiting employees, many jobs are not advertised but are filled through word of mouth. Also many other organisations refer their requirement of hands to some recruitment agencies of repute for directing suitable candidates for interviews and selection. Apart from the above means of filling up vacancies, the candidates themselves advertise, their candidature through internet. The later system of finding out source of job through internet is the modern technique of getting opportunity of gainful employment by the aspirants who are in need of job without loss of time. This is a very useful method of getting employment without much contest from other limited number of candidates.

When getting employment by this method has been made possible and easy, finding out the organisation's working environments, culture and other accurate information is vital for working out the next career move of the Manager intending to switch over. He should use his contacts with friends, colleagues and associates to give him further insight into potential job opportunities.

Also he should have the access of website of the organisation to see how they project themselves. Reading material published by the organisation will help the aspirant for managerial post know about their current priorities, policies and plans.

It is also important for the Manager to decide what type of organisation he prefers for his employment where he can think of his progress in relation to his type of experience he has gathered. He will be able to make pick and choose of taking up employment with an organisation when he will be fortunate enough to get offers of employment from 2/3 organisations simultaneously either through website or internet. In order to determine his right career he should consider the sector, size and structure of different workplaces.

Salary structures of different organisations vary. When a Manager has to think of switch over to other organisation on account of compelling circumstances, his salary criterion is not the main factor. While it is alright that his salary will be equal or more than what he is presently drawing, he should bargain with the higher Management of the new organisation to fix up his salary at certain level commensurate with his experience of working and the present salary drawn by him, if they offer a bit lesser salary.

Self-Esteem

41

A Manager must be a person of self-esteem. Self-esteem is defined as the way a Manager knows himself thoroughly. An ambitious Manager with high self-esteem will accept jobs with entire responsibility. A successful Manager has the following distinguishing features:

(a) He has positive attitude,

(b) He has sense of responsibility,

(c) He has conviction,

(d) He makes the employees ambitious and motivated,

(e) He has confidence,

(f) He has self-interest,

(g) He has understanding,

(h) He is disciplined,

(i) He has sensitivity,

(j) He has modesty.

Possession of all the above traits by a Manager is the result of his being a person of self-esteem. Self-esteem is, therefore, very important for a Manager. For his self-esteem he also gets respects from all and sundry for which he gets impetus to work with intense ardour and efficiency.

Following are the behavioural patterns of a Manager who has no self-esteem.

(a) He is a man of peculiar nature,

(b) He is self-centered,

(c) He is not willing to accept responsibility,

(d) He suffers from egoism,

(e) He is in the habit of making excuses of his own failures,

(f) His behaviour becomes erratic,

(g) He avoids to mix up with people.

Therefore, a Manager without self-esteem is a misfit in the organisation and hence he cannot be a successful Manager in the discharge of his duties—nay he is not at all worthy to cling to Managerial position without having self-esteem.

From what has been discussed in the foregoing, self-esteem is one of the essential ingredients of a Manager who wants to be successful in the discharge of his duties.

Expressing Words of Appreciation

42

It is the psychological tendency of the employees that whenever they are rewarded with the words of appreciation from the Manager for the jobs performed by them to the atonement of the Management, they are enkindled with enthusiasm and inspiration and that they are devoted and inclined to do more jobs in better ways. Expression of words of appreciation by the Manager is thus a motivation for the employees. In this connection, it is worthwhile to mention the saying of the psychologist, William James said that—"One of the deepest desires of human beings is the desire to be appreciated."

For the good jobs done by the employees, the Manager has to express his feelings of appreciation in the following manner:

(a) The way the job has been handled by you is superb and commendable. Please continue to make efforts that the jobs to be done by you in future should also be performed in like manner.

(b) The expression of appreciation from the Manager must be sincere and from the core of heart and not from mouth. It should also not be a flattery.

(c) While expressing the words of appreciation the word, 'but' should not be used, as in the case of the sentence—"I do appreciate your handling the job in most efficient manner but", i.e. to be more precise the word 'but' is not to be used. Otherwise, it will be an appreciation with condition.

(d) The Manager should bear in mind that expressing the words of appreciation does not mean that he has to get the compliment from the employees in return, i.e. "Thank you, sir for your appreciating me".

This is all about the words of appreciation in the case of the jobs done by the employees successfully for the purpose of rejuvenating their spirit.

Managers know it well that "to err is human". Hence, it is not expected from the employees that they will be able to do flawless job all the times, in such case, the Manager should inspire them and appreciate their attempts, although they have not been successful in doing the job. The Manager should say, "Failure is the pillar of success and you should not get dejected". By such exhortation from the Manager the employees will not be down-hearted and that they will be earnest in their future course of working.

It is expedient that the Managers should not throw cold water upon the employees for their failure to do the job on any occasion but exhort and appreciate their attempt. Expressing words of appreciation to the employees is a part of duty on the part of a successful Manager, because he has to work with the employees whose collective endeavour is essential in the interest of the organisation.

How to Think of Attaining Economy by Avoiding Wasteful Expenditures

43

A Manager who is an integral part of an organisation and on whose working the higher Management has complete trust and confidence, has to see how to attain all-round economy by avoiding wasteful expenditure. This is absolutely necessary for efficient running of the organisation. When the margin of profit of the organisation is pretty high resulting in slashing down of the overall expenses the organisation can only march forward to rapid development by way of diversification. This is possible when the Manager takes interest in avoiding wasteful expenditures of the organisation.

There are number of ways as to how wasteful expenditures could be avoided for which the Manager has to see that—

(a) Attachment of Company's cars should be limited to certain executives/officials in consideration of their importance and usefulness to the organisation. Maintenance of log book is a must in order to gauge the personal use of the cars beyond office hours. This will reduce expenses on cars.

(b) Expenses for outside trips undertaken by the executives/officials on company's business should be strictly as per the prescribed rules of the Company.

(c) Too much of fringe benefits allowed to the employees must be marginalised.

(d) There should be proper manning for working in every department according to which appointments of employees are to be made so that application of VRS is not felt a necessity subsequently entailing payment of substantial amount which will have extra burden on the company.

(e) Salary/wages structure should be worked out depending upon the size and profitability of the organisation.

(f) For the employees other than those covered under E.S.I., the Company should go for medi-claim for certain amount in respect of the individual employees depending upon the quantum of their monthly salaries. This will exonerate the Company to make bulk payment of medical expenses to the employees who may be hospitalised for serious ailments.

(g) The Manager has to see that payment of donation is restricted to bare minimum.

(h) While it is the practice of the union leaders to submit to the Management capricious and unreasonable charter of demands, it is the responsibility of the Manager to bargain tactfully with them to come to terms reasonably in the matter of fixation of revised salary/wages structure and other financial implications so that the financial burden on the company is lessened in respect of making payment of Provident Fund contributions increased amount of bonus, gratuity, leave travel concessions, retirement benefits, etc. etc.

(i) Personal use of telephone in the office by the employees should be restricted.

(j) There should be rational use of electricity. In this connection, there should be standing instruction that whenever any officer leaves his chamber, electricity should be put off.

(k) Double increments to the employees in special cases should be given on pragmatic basis, for which the recommendations of the departmental heads should be given due consideration.

(l) Unnecessary paper work should be avoided as also correspondence so as to reduce postage expenses as also stationery which are very high.

The above are the important heads which could be tapped for the purpose of possible reduction of expenses thereby ensuring the organisation to run economically and the Manager has to find his ways to implement the same and here lies his success and competence for the position he clings.

44

Maintenance of Good Relations with the Higher Management and Execution of Policy Matters

Trustworthiness of a Manager in the eyes of the higher Management depends upon his honesty, integrity and sincerity and this ensures establishment of cordial relations between the higher Management and the Manager. It is incumbent on the part of a Manager to know what are the factors which build trust. They are—

(a) A Manager should have openness of mind,
(b) He should have ability and attitude to serve,
(c) He should be a person of good character,
(d) He must have integrity which is the ingredient to trust,
(e) He must have consistency in his deeds and words,
(f) He should have politeness,
(g) He has to give due respect which shows his caring attitude.

It will be in the fitness of things if a Manager is in the know what are the factors which hinder maintenance of good relationship with the higher Management, They are—

(a) Lack of courtesy,
(b) Arrogance in attitude,

(c) Inconsistent behaviour,

(d) Lack of discipline,

(e) Negative attitude,

(f) Uncaring attitude,

(g) Lack of integrity,

(h) Voracious appetite for money.

When a Manager will be in the know that the above factors are standing in the way of building trust with the higher Management, he has not to indulge in resorting to such acts in his own interest. There are people whom we love but we do not trust. So, trustworthiness is a greater compliment than love.

This is all about the explanation as to how a Manager has to create trust and good relationship with the higher Management. Now, the following are the analyses as to how a Manager has to deal with the higher Management for execution of policy matters, duly framed by them.

A Manager has to work under the suzerainty of higher Management. Maintenance of interaction with them is an absolute necessity for a Manager to work in an organisation. He has to execute the policies of the higher Management without contradiction. A Manager has to hold parleys with them at regular intervals and give nod to the policies framed by them without arguments and disagreements. He may, however, put forward his own opinion if he has to say anything in the matter and that too with civility and humility, so that there may not be any rupture and/or misunderstanding in the relations between the higher Management and the Manager. Otherwise, the Manager will not feel plain sailing in the discharge of his duties and that his mind will be tormented always which may affect his continuance in the organisation. It is of course the entire responsibility of the Manager to work in the best interest of the organisation and hence any wrongs in the policies of the higher Management, if there be any, should be mentioned with humility by the Manager, so that the higher Management gives a second thought to the policies framed by them. This way of putting forward his opinion will deepen relations between the higher Management and the Manager and he will gain confidence of the higher Management thus paving the way for his future prosperity. A Manager has to ensure that he must not argue with the higher Management on any matter under any circumstances and on any occasion.

A Manager is to be Hard Working

45

Nothing is impracticable without strenuous labour. A Man is crowned with success in his efforts when he puts in hard labour. Man is elevated to prominence and high position by dint of his vigorous work. Industry is the mother of success. Today is the age of cut-throat competition and survival of the fittest. There is no substitute for hard work. Idling away time brings misery and misfortune. Prosperity and self-development of a person are achieved through hard work only. In service career also employees ascend to high position by strenuous labour.

One cannot develop a capacity to do anything without hard work, "The harder you work, the luckier you get"—says Henry Ford. Success of a person does not come by accident. Everything that we enjoy is the result of hard work. Hard work makes a person better at whatever he is doing. Great talent without will-power and hard work is a waste. There is no magic wand for success. Excellence is not luck? it is the result of a lot of hard work and practice.

It is crystal clear that when hard work is the panacea for attaining success, a Manager who is saddled with responsible and trustworthy jobs cannot resort to easy going habits and show laxity in the discharge of his duties, otherwise, he will be a complete failure as a Manager. Success of a Manager as analysed above depends upon strenuous labour and he will enjoy the laurels of his exalted position. A hard working Manager is a very happy person and feels relieved of his duties, because by his hard work he can always keep the work up-to-date. Accumulation of work is caused by his easy going habits for which he feels mentally disturbed and he cannot do justice to the organisation through his work as Manager.

By virtue of hard work a Manager can excel in any obstacles which he may face during the course of his working and he will be crowned with success as Manager. A Manager can make things look easy when he has mastered the fundamentals of hard work. When a Manager is accustomed with hard work he forgets what is idle time and leisure time. The harder a Manager works, the better he feels; and the better he feels, the harder he works, in the real world, success comes to doers, not to observers.

Hence, the success of a Manager depends upon how much time he puts in doing hard work.

Knowledge of Labour Matters

46

A Manager working in administration ought to have knowledge of the principles of labour laws, although there may be Personnel Manager/Labour officer in the organisation, whose function is to deal exclusively with the labour matters. Question arises—for what purpose the Manager should have knowledge of labour matters. There is of course no compulsion that the Manager in administration shall have to undergo course of personnel management. Administration is a department which deals with the manpower as also HRD in an organisation leaving aside other issues of importance. Administration and the employees are inter-connected and inseparable. In absence of employees administration is practically meaningless. Welfare and problems of the employees are the look-out of administration. Trouble-free running of an organisation depends largely upon the complacence of the employees and this complacence is related to the worthy and competent administration of the Manager.

Trade Unionism is a right of the employees, as stipulated in the Indian Constitution. Labour union in an organisation is formed in order to counteract the unscrupulous and mal-administration of an organisation. A Manager has, therefore, to decipher the sentiments of the employees as to why they have turned violent and ventilated their grievances compelling them to form union, which is happening in many of the organisations. Instances are plenty that many organisations are conspicuous by its absence of labour unions and the employees are working for longer hours in the best interest of the organisation without any resentment. This is due to good governance of the organisation which depends much upon the way of administering the affairs of the Manager.

A Manager should bear in mind always that trouble-free running of the organisation lies mostly with the style of working of the Manager and not with the Personnel Manager/ Labour Officer, because policy matters concerning the employees of the organisation are dealt with by the administration. The Personnel Manager/Labour officer has to extend his hand of cooperation with expert advice to the administration in the matter.

An Administrative Manager has to get himself conversant at least with the following as far as labour matters are concerned for the purpose of maintaining administration.

(a) Provisions of Industrial Disputes Act with subsequent amendments,

(b) Trade Union Act,

(c) Procedure for retrenchment/lay off of the employees,

(d) Procedure for holding domestic enquiry against the charge-sheeted employee, if the charges levelled against him are grievious,

(e) Formalities to be observed with the Labour Directorate in dealing with labour matters,

(f) Issuance of appointment letters to the employees in such a way that there may not be incorporation of any clause therein which will go against the interest of the organisation in case when dispute may arise with regard to employment.

These are the fundamental principles of labour matters a Manager has to know. Apart from the above, the Manager has to get himself conversant with other labour matters by discussions with the Personnel Manager/Labour Officer from time to time. A Manager being in administration has also to take part in the bipartite/tripartite discussions with the leaders of Labour Union separately or combinedly with the Labour Directorate, so that he can also express his views in the matter of settlement of disputes.

It is, therefore, amply clarified that a successful Manager in administration has to get himself involved invariably with labour matters for the purpose of maintaining viability in his administration although there is Personnel Manager/Labour Officer in the organisation.

Maintaining Good Relations with all the other Departmental Managers

47

Managers are the pillars of an organisation. All Managers of different departments/sections are equal in the eyes of the higher Management. They have direct rapprochement with them in respect of their departmental workings. Working in unison and with an attitude of cooperation and healthy relation by the Managers stirs prosperity of an organisation. The word, 'Manager' itself shows that no Manager—whether he is at the helm of affairs of administration, sales or accounts or any other departments is above any of the Managers in official status. If there is any rift in the relations amongst the Managers it does not speak high of the organisation and the employees will mock at and neglect their work. Spirit of working must be upheld in the organisation by creating good working environment by all the Managers. During lunch break all the Managers should enjoy taking their lunch together in any of the office chambers in an atmosphere of good-will and friendship. This will exhibit their freeness of mind which is very important to work together in an organisation without any conflict and bearing in mind that they are the members of a same family.

It is very important that a Manager has to build confederation in maintaining cordial relations with other officers of the organisation. Even a powerful Manager will fish out of water if he has sordid relations with other officers of the organisation. A Manager gets cooperation when he has built up cosy and sweet relations with other officers. Unity is strength which has to be preserved. There is a saying, "To have friends, be a friend". A Manager maintaining cordial relations with other officers will also be in the good books of the higher Management. A Manager has to bear in mind the following ingredients to establish cordial relations with other officers of the organisation.

(a) He should maintain courtesy,

(b) His behaviour should not be inordinate,

(c) He should not have self-centeredness,

(d) He should have cooperative attitude,

(e) He should have amiable disposition,

(f) He should give due respect to other officers,

(g) He should not have negative attitude,

(h) His nature should not be suspicious,

(i) He should have a sense of compassion.

The above are the principal factors upon which positive relationship with other officers of the organisation is built.

Other Traits of a Successful Manager

48

A successful Manager must have the following traits:

Uprightness

A Manager must possess moral integrity. On no occasion he should be hypocritical. His actions and deeds must be straightforward. He must be honest to himself. He should keep himself engaged in constructive activities with positive attitude and straightforwardness.

Mingling with the people of good quality

A Manager has to form an association of persons with high moral character and virtuous quality. By mingling with such people his mental make-up will be moulded in such a fashion that he will be a person of exaltation, which is absolutely desirable befitting to his managerial position. George Washington has said, "Associate yourself with people of good quality if you esteem your reputation, for it is better to be alone than to be in bad company".

Misrepresentation of truths and exaggeration of facts

In the eyes of the higher Management a Manager is a trusted and reliable person on whom responsibilities and many confidential matters of the company are entrusted with. Therefore, a Manager must not entertain hypocrisy and take such action which will go against the interest of the organisation. Otherwise, his position in the organisation will be shaky. Distortion, misrepresentation and exaggeration of facts are not to be entertained by him so that he can continue to enjoy the confidence of the higher Management, which is hard to build. A Manager is to cherish the idea that the confidence he gains from the higher Management is his asset.

Patience

A Manager is saddled with load of work. If he becomes ruffled to handle the spate of work, he is an utter failure to work in managerial position. A Manager must be undaunted and accept things easy. In such case, patience of a Manager plays an important role. With patience he can overcome any insurmountable problem and remain free from scarce and anxieties. Patience is a virtue.

Abstention from criticism

A Manager indulging in criticising others cannot be considered a respectable person. Habit of criticism speaks of the parochial mindedness of a Manager. He cannot draw respect from his subordinates also. As a Manager when respectability is lost everything is lost which is hard to regain. A Manager is a distinguished person. If he is in the habit of criticising others he cannot be treated in high esteem and it is meaningless for such a person to work in managerial position. A Manager should, therefore, abstain from criticising others in the interest of upholding his position in the organisation. He will also draw respect from the higher Management when he is not indulging in criticising others.

Quality of forgiveness

Forgiveness is a great quality of a Manager. By his such quality he can keep the employees under his fold. No man is perfect. He has to commit mistakes because to err is human. It does not speak well that the Manager should go on censuring the employees always for the wrongs committed, rather he should educate them by showing the ways as to how commission of wrongs is to be annulled. When a Manager forgives the erring employees it displays highness of his mind. A successful Manager should, therefore, infuse in himself the quality of forgiveness.

Remaining jovial

A Manager has to remain jovial and humourous. This will keep his mind light and free from anxieties which will help him to accomplish even the intricacies of work with ease and comfort. Success of a Manager depends upon his competence in performing work in apple-pie order when his mind remains undisturbed. His undisturbed mind is the result of his remaining joyous.

Endurance

Endurance is one of the qualities of a Manager. He must be steady and firm under any odds and ends. Lack of steadfastness as well as firmness is a weakness on the part of a Manager. A successful Manager should have endurance to do justice to his work.

Amiable disposition

A person of amiable disposition is endeared by all. Amiable disposition of a Manager helps immensely to attain success in the discharge of his duties as he gets unstinted cooperation from all for his amiable disposition.

Clean and peaceful atmosphere

A Manager has to ensure clean and peaceful atmosphere in the office. This will entice the employees falling in love with office work which in effect will improve their attendance. This will also generate enthusiasm in the minds of the employees to work with efficiency and zeal. A Manager should not unnecessarily inject tension in the minds of the employees. The employees should be kept peaceful always. If their minds are disturbed work will suffer. This should be another stratagem of a Manager as to how the employees should think of work only in such clean and peaceful atmosphere.

Having some knowledge of working of other departments

Although an Administrative Manager has not to interfere in the working of other departments, yet he should have some knowledge of their working, especially of Accounts, because working of this department is directly or indirectly connected with administration. When financial viability is there in an organisation, upholding of sound and strong administration will be made possible and the credibility of the Manager managing the affairs will be augmented.

Attending to outside visitors

Outside visitors calling on the Manager are to be attended too without keeping them waiting outside his office chamber. If, however, there is some delay at times to entertain them because of his engagement with some urgent work necessitating its immediate disposal or his involvement with urgent discussion with someone, the concerned visitors are to be informed by his attendant to make it convenient to wait a bit. While attending to the visitors the Manager has to show pleasant attitude and discuss matters with open heart. But, at the same time, he should not necessarily pass on all the information he has. He should think about what will happen afterwards. If all the information is expressed frankly, if the Manager is presenting information to a senior person, he should not go into more detail than what he needs. The Manager should communicate in the most effective style. Too much information or jargon should be avoided.

Learning from experience

A competent Manager has to think about how to make the best use of his experience. He has to learn lessons from his past actions.

He should realize that if he stops learning, he will soon stop being effective. He has to recognize that the business climate in which the organisation operates changes continuously and he has also to adapt himself with the changed situation. A Manager has to keep himself abreast of the requirements of the organisation from him and to assess their levels of satisfaction with his performance. The pressures of modern business life mean that he can never relax and thinks that he is working as effectively as possible. Always he should be on the look-out for ways to improve. Remember, he has to change as fast as the business world is changing. He should think how he could improve processes in future. He should work out how he is going to achieve an objective.

Work-load of a Manager

Heavy work-load of a Manager impairs his working efficiency and he will falter at times taking judicious decisions. If his work-load is too heavy, he should talk to his senior Manager. The problem could be solved by delegating tasks. Working efficiency of a Manager will increase rather than go down if he takes regular breaks from intense activity. Taking annual leave for 15 days or so for going to a place of interest for change is also recommended. A Manager saddled with responsible work to perform should have nutritious breakfast so that he is able to start the day feeling full of energy and ready to face the most difficult tasks. During the day he should take breaks to recharge his batteries so as to enable him to work at his optimum efficiency. Cigarette smoking saps vitality. A Manager should, therefore, eschew smoking which will keep him always fit to work. Also a healthy balanced diet will invigorate him to face the challenges of modern life. A Manager who has to maintain his effectiveness should take 15/20 minutes break in the middle of the day during working hours to prepare himself for the challenges of the afternoon work.

Building confidence

A Manager should be a man of confidence. He should believe in himself and his abilities to do any work successfully assigned to him. He will feel sure that he will find solutions to any problem and feel good about outcomes. Any belief to the contrary will reduce his confidence. This means that if he believes that he is a poor decision maker he will feel unconfident about decisions. In such case, he will feel shaky in taking any decision and this will not make him worthy to work as Manager. Inner confidence enables the Manager to make decisions and take actions that help him sustain a healthy work-life balance. The greater is his confidence, the greater is his capacity to take correct actions and succeed at life and work. He should adopt a "can-do" mentality and he will achieve his goals. He should learn to value and believe in himself, build on his strength and aim to be resourceful and decisive. The way he views himself is expressed in his posture and his body language. When he behaves confidently, people will follow his lead. A happy and balanced life starts with self-belief and vision.

Improving working relations

Managers need high levels of interpersonal skills to achieve top performance in working environments. Successful Managers need to achieve top results from their teams. In the teamwork when results are not up to the standard the staff should not be blamed. Instead, the Manager should recognize the part he plays in the results they produce. He is to imagine alternative approaches that might work better next time. A Manager should spend on an average ten minutes on the team of employees to give guidance for doing the work assigned to them. What he says in this time is crucial to overall performance and results. The language for giving guidance and advice should be clear-cut and without ambiguity.

Interviewing candidates by a Manager

When a Manager is one of the members of an Interview Board, his way of interviewing candidates is important. He should ask questions designed to get interviewees to respond in an interesting, illuminating, lively, animated or entertaining way. Rigorous or aggressive questioning may be encountered by the interviewees which will not speak good for the organisation as its maintaining reputation. A Manager should decide in advance prior to taking interviews what he is willing to say and what he will not reveal. No interviewees should be exhaustively pressured to face questions voley after voley. The way of expression of the interviewee and his etiquette is a clear testimony whether he is suitable for the post he has applied for.

Letter writing

Correct and appropriate way of writing letters by a Manager is an art. His mental make-up and store of knowledge are evidently expressed through the letters he writes. Letters should be to the point. Jargon-free writing is known as "plain English". By such letter the readers will not feel confused and irksome. It features short, everyday words and brief sentences. Unnecessary technical terms and officialese are avoided. Plain

English follows a clear and logical order that takes into account the needs and interests of the readers. Letters should be straightforward and transparent and not pompous and verbose. Use of idioms and phrases should be avoided. In the letters using contractions such as "you're" and "we'll: should be avoided. Also instead of using passive voice letters should contain active voice. Letters should be written in such a way that the readers feel comfortable to read. A Manager in his letter should use concise words such as "now" rather than "at this point of time". Letters need to be polite because they represent the good image of the organisation.

Maintaining confidentiality of matters

A Manager has to deal with many confidential matters of an organisation. Preservation of the same speaks of his integrity and the trust he gets from the highest echelon of the Management. Preservation of confidential matters of an organisation cannot be expected of a fickle minded Manager. On account of absent mindedness and liberality of attitude if confidential matters are given vent to by a Manager, it will have a great deal of damage to the organisation and his services will be at stake. Managers are the trusted employees and they have to work as such to gain confidence of the higher Management.

Self-understanding

Self-understanding of a Manager and what he wants to achieve enable him to lead a fulfilling life. He should be sensitive to his emotions, assess his priorities and plan action. He should use his beliefs, perceptions, choices and actions in strategic ways to reach the balance he needs. He should think positively and take responsibility for his choices and decisions. He should have beliefs about everything including work, life, success and happiness. These beliefs influence his choices and actions. A Manager is responsible for the choices that he makes and he can take control of his work. He should always consider the consequences of his choices for himself and others. He should remember that his actions not only affect him but affect those around him too.

Understanding emotional intelligence

By improving emotional intelligence a Manager can enjoy greater happiness, success in his relationships, his life and his work. Development of his emotional intelligence enhances his power of decision-making and helps him communicate more honestly, think more clearly and act more authentically. He should be aware of that his feelings are a gateway to creativity, intuition and inspiration. Emotional intelligence helps him develop understanding and trust in his relationships. Monitoring his thoughts and feelings can help him see how well he is balancing his work and life.

Taking time to participate in sports

Taking time to participate in sports will help a Manager keep him healthy and fresh in mind so that he is ready to face new challenges in office. He has to remain fresh and healthy, free from exhaustion/sleeplessness and impaired relationships. A healthy amount of leisure can enrich his activity at work, his time at home and his friendships in life. Membership of Lions Club or any other important club will help a Manager develop his mental faculty by his communing with the galaxy of intellectuals at the club in the evening after office hours.

Taking allocated annual leave

A Manager is no doubt saddled with pressure of work throughout the year which necessitates respite to regain vigour and strength to devote to his working with efficiency. While an organisation prescribes annual leave for the purpose that it cannot normally require its employees to work continuously throughout the year through stress and strains, a Manager has to avail of the same for going to a place of health resort by taking annual leave to invigorate his health and energy in order to work with renewed vigour, strength and efficiency after his return from leave.

Need for simplification of the life of a Manager

Success has traditionally been defined as "possession of more"—more money with substantial bank balance, high priced car, a job with more responsibility, a good house to live, a social life with more friends. A Manager should realize that too much of "more" can clutter up his life and he may feel restlessness. All these things can leave him over-stretched, over committed and overwhelmed. A Manager should, therefore, let go of excesses and focus on what is most essential for him. He should evaluate his real priorities. To sum up, a Manager has to lead a simplified life to be free from all scarce and anxieties.

Forgetting office work after leaving office

A Manager should leave his work behind after leaving the office. He should clearly realize what is "work time" and what is "family time". When office work is over he should switch off the same and stop thinking about it. It has been observed that a handful number of Managers set to do office work after returning homes. Home is an ideal place for relaxation. A Manager needs relaxation after day's work. It is not at all desirable that he should again devote to work at home neglecting the company of his family members. Man is not a machine. Even a machine needs rest. He should aim to live more and work better. When he leaves office each evening he should switch his mind off from his work. He should take time to rejuvenate and he will feel refreshed and better equipped to deal with work the next day.

Maintaining rapport with staff members

Creating a sense of belonging to the organisation by the staff members is one of the very important tasks of a Manager. By this, the staff members will always feel inclined to attend office regularly and punctually and that they will work so closely and with devotion that they will feel it is their own job they are performing. Organisations prosper when employees work sincerely. Sincerity in the working of the employees is the responsibility of the Manager. It depends upon how a Manager acts upon the staff members. He has to ensure that the staff members work with team-spirit and joviality of mind. He has to realize that his success as a Manager is dependent on the help and cooperation of others. Staff members should be made to feel that they are treated without discrimination by the Manager and that every staff member is equal in the eyes of the Manager. Their personal problems are heard and if any staff member is in urgent need of money to defray his unforeseen commitment, he should be awarded with financial help by the organisation. No employee should be coerced to work with red eyes of the Manager. Employees should be made to feel that there is no difference of feeling of the Manager—both outside and inside. This will create respectability to the Manager by the employees.

Overcoming difficulties

A Manager is likely to be fraught with difficult situations at times during the course of his working in office. Be it known to him that everyone experiences bad times. But he should have toughness of character to overcome the same. It is important for him that he should not be nervous and tensed when he is faced with challenges. In the difficult situation a Manager should hold his nerve and stay positive so that his attitude does not make a difficult situation worse. He should keep his mind upbeat. He should not feel demotivated during difficult times else this will create negativity. He should adopt positive qualities that will bring him success.

Focussing on the aims of a Manager

A Manager has to decide what are his objectives and begin to separate what he must do now to achieve these objectives from any other matters. The more specific and clear he makes his objectives the more focussed his work will be. He should never involve himself doing unnecessary work which is not within the purview of his working as a Manager. Such work is to be distracted from his real responsibilities. He should distinguish between the actions that directly contribute to his business success and the other issues that infringe on his workload, which burdens him unnecessarily. He should work out his objectives by listing the key areas of his job in order of importance.

Avoiding delay in taking action

Action now is often more effective than action later. A Manager has to make sure that his decision is based on a good understanding of the facts and in that case he has to take action without any delay.

It is argued that if action is delayed it is denied. A Manager has to prepare a to-do list of matters which need action to be taken. He will go through the list and in order of importance he will prioritise taking action of the matter. He should remember that by his methodical way of working as in the case of taking action he will not feel irksome in his working—whatever it may be complicated and critical. An urgent action is one that needs to be done now, but an important action is one that is vital to achieving his objectives. A Manager should take immediate and decisive action whenever possible, but not act immediately if he is unclear how to choose the right option.

Structuring of time

Time of a Manager is precious. Having been saddled with pressure of work shouldering higher responsibilities in the discharge of his duties, he can least afford to misuse time. For him time is money. While engaging himself in discussion with others in the office relating to the matters of the organisation, allocation of his time is important. He cannot lengthen his time beyond what is necessary, else he will be fraught with difficult situation to perform his other work and the entire work will be in disarray. A competent and successful Manager must be time-conscious. Reckless use of time during working hours will not help him do justice to the job assigned to him. He should also maintain lunch time strictly according to allocated time in order to energise him from fatigue.

Leading a balanced life

Leading a reckless life by a Manager is not at all desirable. Disciplined way of leading life by him will systematise his working which will bring peace of mind. Indisciplined life disturbs his working. If a Manager wants to continue to build on and develop his efficiency at work, it is important to maintain a healthy balance between work and leisure. Leading a balanced life keeps a man healthy. There is increasing evidence that people who are physically fit can cope with the challenges of modern business life. If the working efficiency of a Manager is to be intensified, he should take periodical breaks from intense activity. A Manager should desist from taking alcoholic drinks, because taking the same will be a cause of his intoxication which will impair his ability to take effective decisions. A healthy and balanced diet will give him energy to face the challenges of modern life.

Giving pause in the working

A Manager is supposed to work in the office for more than eight hours a day on account of his dealing with many important matters of the organisation. He is not to leave the office along with other employees. If done so, it looks odd. Ceaseless working without short break makes him weary which impairs his smooth working. When a Manager is required to respond to challenges, he should learn to stay calm by practising relaxation for a short while intermittently during the course of his working. He has to retain his composure so that he is better able to deal with any difficult situation that may crop up. Shouting in the office for the wrongs committed by any employee is never recommended. This proves his intolerable attitude, which is not expected of a Manager.

How to create impact on others

The way a Manager presents himself in his dress he puts on and in his body language creates an impression with others about him. He should make a good impression by dressing to match the business culture. He should choose well fitted suits in quality materials. He should make sure that he feels confident and relaxed in what he wears. People tend to form their first impression with a Manager immediately on meeting him. People will be guided by costume, voice, handshake and facial expressions of the Manager. First impression—whether it is good or bad is difficult to do away with. A Manager has to notice the impact he makes on others with the help of his influencing skills. If he takes care of his appearance he will create a favourable impression with the people and he will be seen as a reliable person by them. When getting with people the Manager should ask how they are and also enquire how their families are.

Influencing senior Managers

A Manager has to work to gain the respect of his senior Managers. He should impress upon them with his ability to handle responsibilities with success and in this way he can get their confidence on him. While influencing senior Managers, he should consider their interests and make them adopt his proposals accordingly. Senior Managers take a long-term idea as to how the business and the organisation can grow in future and they start working accordingly and assess the impact on the organisation as a whole. The Manager should show that he has considered these matters also. He should try to present novelty of ideas for acceptance by the senior Managers. A Financial Manager is primarily concerned with accounting of the organisation. He should also involve himself in the long-term business development. A Manager has to see that his ideas are evaluated. If a Manager is not in consonance with any of the ideas of a senior Manager he should put forward his argument mildly with reasonings.

Doing away with bad habits

Shouting in the office every now and then disturbing the peaceful atmosphere and bad behavioral pattern of a Manager hurting the sentiments of the employees are among his bad habits. Bad habits prevent a Manager from getting things done with ease. He is ought to be loveable and respected by the employees by his amiable nature. He should know how to change his bad habits for having effectiveness in his working. He should admit his own weaknesses which hinder him from achieving the highest standards. Habits are of course the second nature of a person and it poses a great problem to do away with the same easily.

In his own interest for becoming an effective Manager he must eschew his bad habits. It is to be borne in mind by a Manager that all top performers have spent years building the habits of success. When he feels that his bad habits are no longer getting the results he wants, his prime objective will be to shun his bad habits. No person likes that a Manager should shout in the office and resort to bad behaviour. This is his dark side as a Manager. No employee wants that he will be adorned with bad behaviour and shouting by the Manager in the office. This dries up their working spirit.

Use of language to influence others

Use of effective language by a Manager is very important to get good results. A Manager should take care of that his staff members and others are not hurt by the discourteous language he uses. He must be soft spoken. Staff members will be inclined to work whole-heartedly by the sweet language he uses. Sweet language is an effective tool to inspire people. Even when a Manager is in pensive mood due to some reason or the other, he should not lose control of himself while speaking with others with his soft language. Use of soft and sweet language is an art. Success of a Manager in his working depends upon the words he uses spiced with softness and sweetness. When he can get the affinity of the employees by his words he is no doubt a successful Manager. Employees will not hesitate to do any work when they are endeared by the soft and sweet language of the Manager.

Reviewing performance during the last 24 hours

In order to assess success and failures in the discharge of his duties during the last 24 hours, a Manager should review the key incidents so as to enable him to know where he stands to fulfil the desired results as Manager. By this assessment he will be able to know his weaknesses which debarred him from achieving good results. While he should not be upset in his failures to attain desired results, he has to be meticulous and cautious to handle matters in future so that he has not to meet with failures while doing any complicated work. When he will be able to know his weak points he will look at always to develop his performance, as he knows that personal and professional development is critical to success in business. He should spend 5-10 minutes every day for his assessment work.

A Manager is not to embroil himself in confrontation

Confrontation with others robs of peace of mind of a Manager which completely upsets him in his working. It is, therefore, always wise to avoid confrontation with difficult persons to remain peaceful, confrontation torments the mind which is a retrogression to work in effective way. There are certain persons who believe in motive hunting of a motiveless malingnity, as in the words of Iago of Shakespeare's book, *Othelo*. Their main objective is to see the fun by intoxicating the peaceful temper of a Manager so as to discredit him in the eyes of the higher Management. The Manager should never be beguiled by the ill-motive of such persons in the office. If any person shows any unruly behaviour he should not be paid in his own coin. In such situation, the best course left with the Manager will be that he walks away in order to cool down the angry feeling. This is the best way to tackle with such unruly and difficult persons. Primary objective of a Manager will be to gain cooperation of difficult people so that they can understand their folly to confront with the Manager practically with no tangible reason.

Pursuing self-development by a Manager

A Manager himself is responsible for his own career development. Accordingly, he has to plan in what way he should mould his career development in future, so that he can attain complete confidence in himself that he will not face any problem whatsoever in getting gainful employment even in the cut-throat competitive employment market. The distinct advantage for the persons who take their own development with right earnest is that they are more confident about their own abilities. For attaining personal development the Manager should do the following:

(a) He should equip himself by reading books that interest him in his professional development,

(b) He should form habits of reading professional journals to keep him abreast of new developments.

(c) He should undertake some short course studies to enhance his knowledge further,

(d) If possible, he should work with a trainer or senior colleague to increase his skills,

(e) He should find ways to acquire new skills at local or corporate access centres,

(f) If the higher Management desires, he can get the opportunity to officiate his higher official when he is on leave for 15 days or more.

Facing the crisis in career development

Career progression can sometimes be thrown off by sudden and unexpected events which may be caused due to being sacked or being found redundant or company merger or take over or any other possible reason. Whatever may be the type of setback a person is likely to lose dignity and is demoralised. Under the circumstances, he should not lose heart but adopt a calm approach to help defuse the difficult situation. He should ensure that it is a short-term setback and it will not affect his long-term prospects. The skills and self-development which he has attained will not go to waste, but will be rewarded again. He should always feel that his skills and self-development are his permanent assets which would be fully utilised in other organisation too. He should keep positive look at all the facts and look for ways to boost his confidence in other areas of his life while he thinks about his next move.

In what way a Manager can influence others

When the ideas of a Manager are heard with patience and accepted, he gets upper hand to exert his influence on others. This is no doubt a plus point on his part by virtue of which he can contribute directly to his ability to attain his prominence as a competent Manager of an organisation. In order to persuade others to adopt his ideas and view-points, he should present a clear case that matches their needs. With this art of influencing others he speaks logically, fluently and confidently. A Manager wins the hearts of the people when he respects their sentiments and aspirations. After influencing others a Manager should be alert to their feelings and adapt what they say. It will not be in the fitness of things that a Manager after being successful in influencing others should dictate terms over them. If done so, he will be alienated from their minds and the respectability will be wanting from the core of their hearts. It is very necessary that after influencing others a Manager should work with productive relationship and collaboration to reach mutually beneficial goals. He should emphasize what he has common with others rather than what divides him. After influencing others a Manager should give opportunity to express their own view-points freely. After listening to the same he should explain his ideas in more detail, if their ideas are short of fulfilment.

Disadvantages for frequent change of organisation

It does not speak high of an experienced Manager to go on changing organisations frequently. Frequent change of organisation is nothing but forming his habit. This shows his unstable mind and there is every likelihood that he has to pay a high price for such habit, as in most of the cases he cannot consolidate his position in any organisation, thereby denying elevation in service. In the initial stage of taking up managerial position, when he has to think of gleaning experience first, he can of course think of switching over to other organisations where different organisational systems are prevalent. This will no doubt augment his confidence to work in different types of organisations under different situations. Such changeover of employment can be done for a maximum period of five years and not beyond that excepting in extraneous circumstances. An experienced Manager has to fix up himself in employment with an organisation of repute where by virtue of his extensive experience he can easily consolidate his position and continue to enjoy the laurels of his exalted position there. The distinct advantage of his continuity in employment in such organisation is that there is abundant scope of his further promotion in service as also he will qualify himself in getting gratuity after completion of five years of service, the amount of which is no doubt substantial. Apart from the above, he can put forward his matured view-points to adopt ways and means for prosperity of the organisation and the higher Management will consider him a magnate for the organisation. In such case, when the government employees think of continuance of their employment till retirement, such experienced Manager can also think of continuance of employment till superannuation with assured future with the organisation. While appearing at interviews the Managers who have developed the habit of moving to and fro cannot convince the interview board about his continuity in employment if selected and in such case the interviewers will give second thought to provide employment to such candidate.

How to improve effectiveness in working

Research has revealed that it is not primarily intelligence quotient (IQ) or technical competence that determine the professional success of a Manager. Professional effectiveness depends upon how the Manager manages himself in different situations and his working relations with others—known as "emotional intelligence". There is increase in the working efficiency when a Manager develops his intelligence skills. There are two aspects of emotional intelligence that determine performance as a Manager. The first is his ability to handle situation in an efficient manner and the second is his ability to be sensitive to the working of others. Emotional intelligence is so important that it transforms the performance and the career of a Manager. A Manager has to recognize that NLP (Neuro-Linguistic Programming) helps him to work with others without any problem and to develop himself. If a Manager feels that he has difficulty in meeting important deadlines, he should use NLP skills of setting his daily objectives so as to enable him to plan his time effectively.

Distinguishing Features of a Manager to Know his Mind

49

There are some distinguishing features of a Manager to know his mind, which are as follows:

(a) A Manager has to maintain eye contact with others at the time of continuing discussions. This establishes his positive rapport with them,

(b) A Manager should have relaxed body language which conveys his confidence to deal with any matter at different situations,

(c) His open jacket without fastening buttons presents an image of honesty and openness of mind,

(d) His open handed gesture indicates integrity,

(e) His confident stance establishes credibility,

(f) He should be flexible in his approach to other people,

(g) While sitting in chair his leaning forward posture shows his attentiveness,

(h) Handshakes with strong hold by a Manager indicate his close affinity of mind, affection and warmth,

(i) When a Manager is with low confidence, his facial muscles are tense and strained,

(j) Proper dressing of hair as well as daily shaving is the embodiment of his smartness. Lengthy hair does not augur well for a Manager,

(k) Jovial mood of a Manager indicates his open mindedness. He is a man of complexity when he looks pensive and remains without smiles always,

(l) Smartness in walking represents his straightforwardness,

(m) When the shoulder of a Manager is leaned forward it shows that he lacks in confidence,

(n) Speedy writing of a Manager with legibility of words speaks of his steadiness of mind.

Need for Evaluating Customers

50

For a commercial organisation it is the prime objective of a Sales Manager to look after the needs of the customers. Customers are the assets of an organisation. In order to make an organisation thrive the Sales Manager has to ensure that he meets their demands and expectations. It is essential that if the Manager has to serve the customers well, there should be thorough understanding of them. He should plan how best the customers are satisfied. The customers who are satisfied are loyal to the organisation. The Manager has to ensure that customers' best interests are maintained for all times. In order to intensify performance of business, the Manager has to effectively meet the requirements of the customers on time. This will repose faith on the organisation as a well-reputable one by the customers. By adopting the policy of customer-first approach, the Sales Manager has to provide right products at reasonable price and best services to the customers. This is vital for long-term profitability of the organisation.

In a changing world consumers' fashions as also the customers' needs are changing constantly. It is, therefore, very necessary that the Manager must give priority in understanding their changing needs and plan how to defray their new requirements. He should hold parleys with them on regular basis to identify their changing needs and offer standard products and best services. In today's business it is the expectation of the customers that they are given first-class services and any dearth of the same will be disappointing to them. The customers know it very well that there is no shortage of competitors dealing with the same type of merchandise they need and hence there is every possibility that they may switch over to other organisations when they will start feeling that customers' needs are not being met with by the organisation with whom they are maintaining their business relations for so long.

The Sales Manager and his team should visit the customers at their premises regularly to keep them apprised of the problems of the customers, if any, and redress the same immediately. Service-after-sales should be one of the prime objectives of the Sales Manager. It will also be his constant endeavour to know the competitors' activities in the market and what is their sales strategy. The Sales Manager has to formulate new policy to woo the customers depending upon the competitors' dealings and activities. No Sales Manager can afford to part with any of his customers in cut-throat competition of the competitors.

All customers—whether big or small must be treated equally so that the small customers are not to think that they are second class customers for the organisation, when their share of contribution for greater profitability is lesser than that of the bigger customers. Some customers may be considered important for an organisation because of their larger off-take but such customers may not be valuable because of their short-term requirements. It is, therefore, necessary that the Manager should make a list of top ten permanent customers who are to be given special treatment and facilities.

Fluctuation in the sale of products is common to every organisation. The Sales Manager is not to be worried of the same. In order to see the quantum of increase and decrease of sale of products every month at a glance he should prepare a graph showing therein the sales figures every month and affix on the wall in front of his seat in the office. If there is downward trend of sales every month, he should analyse the reasons for the same and devise ways and means to arrest such decline in sales.

Complaints of the customers provide opportunities to the Sales Manager to know what are their grievances. When he takes immediate action to redress the same efficiently, the Sales Manager can retain the customers and improve his relationship with them. While handling their complaints the Manager should apologize for the inconvenience caused to them. The customers should be made to realize that their grievances and problems are not unheeded and that the Management gives top priority in resolving matters to their full satisfaction.

There are certain customers who prefer cash payments against delivery of goods to them. The number of such customers are of course limited and their off-take is not voluminous. The Sales Manager has no problem with such customers as far as payment is concerned. It is suggested that the Sales Manager should not agree to deliver goods to petty customers on credit. If done so, there is always risk that the sales proceeds may not be realised from the petty customers whose financial stability is not sound. Such customers may wind up their business at any time and their whereabouts are untraceable which leads to piling up of bad debts for the organisation. This is not unlikely that such situation is the problem with many organizations. If, however, the Sales Manager bills his major customers for bigger amount, he has to consider whether this system benefits them. This should be done as per agreed term. Usually, bigger customers prefer to make payments in regular instalments depending upon their cash flow more effectively before taking next supply.

The Sales Manager has to ensure that delivery schedule of goods is maintained strictly on time so that the customers have not to starve for delay in getting the items ordered for by them. If for any reason beyond the control of the Sales Manager the ordered items are delayed for delivery, the customers are to be informed well in advance about the reason of such delay, so that they suffer minimum disruption. In the event that the customers are not informed, the customers may turn to other organisations for business. This will be a setback for the organisation's reputation. A Manager has to keep in mind about this.

Today's business world is highly competitive. There are many remote places where day-to-day sale is not possible. By the advertisement of the products of the organisation through radios and television in particular, the customers all over the places are directly made conversant with the products, which creates a leaning towards such products in their minds and thus the sale is increased manifold. Not only this, from time to time new products are launched by the organisations and display of such products through television creates an impact in the minds of the customers. Moreover, the Sales Manager has to arrange door-to-door sale of new products to bring such items within the direct reach of the consumers. This way of sale other than advertisement will also evoke positive response. This is no doubt an advanced technique to boost sale of new products.

On account of wrong policy of the Sales Manager a customer may be lost and this will be catastrophic for the organisation, because customers are the assets of an organisation. Therefore, before formulating sales policy the Manager has to use SAFE criteria (Suitable, Acceptable, Feasible and Enduring). SAFE criteria are explained in the following manner.

(a) Is the decision to frame sales policy really the most suitable one, taking into account the current situation of the customers?

(b) Is the decision to frame sales policy underlying certain conditions therein acceptable to the customers?

(c) Will it be feasible and practical to implement the sales policy?

(d) Will the decision endure in the long run or will it be unacceptable to the customers?

In this age of cut-throat competition in business field, maintaining quality of products and good services, which meet the customers' expectation, is of utmost necessity. Even if a certain percentage of increase in the prices of products is felt a necessity, it can be done so, but with convincing reasonings to the satisfaction of the customers. Prices of products which are once fixed taking into account all aspects cannot remain static for all times in future, as with the lapse of years prices of all things are always on the upward trend. The Manager has to ensure that there should be balancing between the increased prices and the quality of the products.

The Manager and his team members should always do right things for the customers. If the customers are misguided by giving wrong information or any mistake is committed by any of the team members detrimental to the interest of the customers, they should be contacted immediately to explain the error instead of waiting for the complaints to be received from the customers. When the Sales Manager of the organisation is providing first-class services, the customers will have faith in the dealings of the Manager and the products he provides. The Manager has to ensure that his team members are working in the most appropriate way to satisfy the customers by their dealings and services. The Manager has to guide and educate his team members as to how they will have to deal with the customers so that no complaints from the customers are received. The Manager should enquire confidentially and diplomatically as to how the customers have got the impression after his team personnel have discussed with them various matters concerning sales. The Sales Manager and his team members must be helpful in solving problems of the customers. The customers should be greeted with smile and in a friendly manner. The Manager and his team members should use positive words and body language to show to the customers that they are valued for the organisation and that they should be thanked for doing business. An important part of relationship-building is to listen to the customers. The Manager should help the team members realize that providing satisfaction to the customers will bring enormous job satisfaction to them.

It is the tendency of most of the customers that they give little time to consider any change suiting to their requirements. In such situation the Manager has to take quick action for change for their benefits, as suggested by them. If the change is gigantic, the Manager has to examine the risks involved and in such case he will request the customers to wait for certain time for its implementation as it is to be worked out by the highest echelon of the Management. The Management has to see what the benefits of the change will be for the customers and also the organisation, but in any case the customers' benefits are to be considered, if not fully/ when the interest of the organisation is impaired.

Effective communication with the customers is very important to keep them satisfied. The Manager has to write his letters to the customers in such a way that it is customer-friendly. The letter should be soothing and polite. It should be easy to understand, concise and to the point. Unnecessary and difficult words should be avoided so that the customers are not confused to read such letters. Business letters are always free from literature English. Regular communication between the organisation and the customers prevent problems to emerge. The Sales Manager makes sure that in all his communications with the customers, he presents them a realistic expectation of the benefits they will get from the organisation in respect of the products and the services.

Organisation thrives in the long run when it keeps pace with the change in market trends and evolving the needs of the customers. The Sales Manager has to ensure that his customers continue to receive advantages from the products and the services he offers to them at all varying stages. Achieving target of sales is a clear indication that the organisation is on way to thriving and this is possible when the customers are fully satisfied with the services rendered to them by the Sales personnel and also with the enlisting of new customers, customers will always show their bent of mind and loyalty to the organisation when they will find it convenient to do business with the organisation. The Sales Manager has to plan his business strategy depending upon the customers' future plan. Knowing in advance what the customers have in mind in future will be helpful for the Sales Manager to find ways to strengthen customer relationships by way of changing his strategy of sales adaptable to the changing needs of the customers. This will help the organisation stand in the cut-throat competition in the market.

All the personnel of the sales team are to be exhorted always so that they take challenge in their working under tribulations which they may face in the discharge of their duties in odds and ends. They have to keep constant touch with the customers to know their problems, if any. This will help maintain perennial business relationship between the organisation and the customers. It will also create weight of the visit of the Sales Manager to them periodically, as the customers will feel that they are evaluated very much in the eyes of the organisation. For the best performance done by any of the sales personnel financial reward by way of ex-gratia payment should be given. This will not only bolster his sales activities further, but also enthuse other sales personnel to emulate his way of performance. Sales personnel who are considered cream of the sales Department should be promoted to the next higher rank so that they are not lured by other organisations to take up employment with them on better terms.

Personality of the Sales Manager with his tenderness in speaking is his plus point to woo the minds of the customers. The Sales Manager and his sales team should be cool minded persons. Customers will reject those who are ruffled in temperament. Business organisation cannot march forward to success when its Sales Manager and sales personnel are not amenable to the reasonings of the customers. Taking one sided and upper hand action without giving weight to the customers' arguments will not be a fruition and the organisation will pay a high price for the same in the long run.

Questions and Answers

51

The job of a Manager is such that he must have broad-based knowledge of his working, for which he must be aware of the important provisions/stipulations. Possession of such knowledge will be conducive for him to work successfully as a Manager. Otherwise, he will have no locus standi to work in such capacity and there is every likelihood that he will meet with failure in the discharge of his duties. I have, therefore, thought it prolific to discuss some of the important provisions/stipulations through questions and answers, as follows, and the Managers must have to keep themselves abreast of the same in their own interest.

Q. 1. After prohibition of Contract Labour system in an organisation, can the workmen legally claim to be employees on regular basis?

Ans. Contract Labour system in an organisation can be prohibited by a Notification under the provision of the Contract Labour (Regulation and Abolition) Act, 1970. From the legal point of view, the workmen working under Contract Labour system cannot claim to be regular employees of the organisation, as they are not the employees of the organisation. If, however, the management of the organisation is desirous of appointing workmen for performing job on regular basis, they are to be given preference in such employment, if they are found suitable for the job.

In this connection, it is of course pertinent to mention here that if the contract for supply of Contract Labour between the contractor and the organisation is deceptive, the workmen could be treated as employees of the organisation by regularising their services, in the event of abolition of Contract Labour system under the afore-said provision.

Q. 2. Is bonus an employee's right? When an organisation is losing, is it obligatory on the part of the owner to pay bonus? What is the difference between statutory bonus and bonus under a private agreement?

Ans. Under Section 1 of the Payment of Bonus Act, 1965, employees of every factory and any establishment employing 20 or more persons on any day in an accounting year, have statutory right to receive bonus, provided they worked for at least 30 working days in an accounting year. Section 36 of the Act empowers the Government to exempt an establishment from the provisions of the Act having regard to certain factors, e.g. financial position thereof. An employee has a right to receive bonus irrespective of the fact whether the employer is making profit or not particularly when the payment of bonus was initiated earlier in the organisation.

Statutory payment of bonus is made as per the Payment of Bonus Act, 1965. On the other hand, the employer and the employees may arrive at an agreement or settlement regarding payment of bonus payable to the employees in line with the provisions of the 1965 Act to determine the minimum quantum of bonus payable.

Q. 3. If a company declares closure of its undertaking, what is the consequence for the employees? What are the remedies open to the employees?

Ans. Section 2(cc) of the Industrial Disputes Act, 1947 defines "closure" as closing down of a place of employment or part thereof. The consequence for the employees is that their services are terminated. If it is a case of genuine closure, the employees are only entitled to notice and compensation as per Section 25-FFF of the 1947 Act. If the undertaking is closed down under unavoidable circumstances, the compensation shall not exceed an employee's three months average pay. Unavoidable circumstances do not include factors like financial difficulties/losses of the employer.

If the closure is a stratagem for a lockout under Section 2(1) of the Industrial Disputes Act, 1947 which means temporary suspension of work to counteract workmen's collective bargaining, the validity of the closure may be challenged before the Industrial Tribunal by the workmen concerned.

Q. 4. At the time of leaving a company an employee has not received his final settlement and in the meantime the company has also changed its name. Under the circumstances, what is the way out to get his due payment from the Company?

Ans. If an employee had left the company without transgressing the terms of employment and also he is legally entitled to get all his dues from the Company, for which they (Company) are dilly-dallying to clear his dues, the employee can always put his claim of getting the dues payable to him by the previous company by filing a civil suit. If the organisation is a government one, he can proceed under Article 226 of the Constitution against the employer. In the matter of getting payment of his dues, it does not matter that the Company has changed its name subsequently.

Q. 5. What should be the recruitment policy for trainees in an organisation other than the trainees as per the Apprentices Act, 1961?

Ans. Trainees are appointed by an organisation not as per the Apprentices Act, 1961 but against permanent vacancies. Apprentices engaged (not appointed) for certain period are not the employees of the organisation, who are debarred from getting all other benefits of the organisation. These trainees/apprentices get some amount of allowance only from the organisation and not salary.

Trainees against regular vacancies are appointed either from the direct applicants or through advertisement in newspaper. For appointing the trainees the candidates are called for interviews after shortlisting the applications. Before appointing the trainees, their references are taken into account as also their medical tests are conducted to consider suitability of the candidates for the posts they are to be appointed. Generally, the trainees against permanent vacancies are appointed for a period of one year and after completion of traineeship the candidates are taken in regular employment fitting in grades as per the status of the employees. The trainees during their training period, unlike the trainees engaged as per the Apprentices Act, 1961, do not enjoy all the benefits similar to what the confirmed employees enjoy.

Q. 6. Is it justified that a Company can issue termination letter to its employees giving three/one months' notice, as the case may be, as stipulated in the appointment letters, without assigning any reason thereof? In such case, can the employee fight it out?

Ans. As per Article 226 of the Constitution, an employee can of course challenge the arbitrary decision of the employer in terminating his services without assigning any reason. This will be in the case of the employee working in public sector company, as such company cannot deal with its employees in arbitrary manner, although in the appointment letter it may be written clearly in one of the clauses that the services of the employee can be terminated after confirmation of his services by giving three/one months' notice or pay in lieu thereof without assigning any reason thereof.

In the case of working in a private limited company, unless the employees are protected under the Industrial Disputes Act, it may not be possible to win success in filing case against the employer in the above situation. The basic reason is that the employee has accepted the terms of employment and the service rules of the Company by signing the duplicate copy of the appointment letter. The only consolation is that such a clause in the appointment letter is contrary to public policy and so it may go in favour of the employees other than working in managerial capacity.

Q. 7. What is contractual service?

Ans. The job on which the employees are engaged for a certain period of years is a contract service. After completion of the contractual service it may not be renewed for a further period or in certain cases when the job necessitates continuity the contractual service may be renewed, contractual service does not attract the retirement benefits like provident fund and gratuity as also other fringe benefits, as in the case of regular employment vis-a-vis the incremental salary. The person engaged on contractual service is not a regular employee of the Company.

Q. 8. In what way the terms of V.R.S. could be amended to make it more effective?

Ans. Voluntary Retirement Scheme (V.R.S.) is called 'Exit Policy' or 'Golden handshake' or 'Separation Scheme'. It is of paramount necessity to make some changes in V.R.S. policy to get overwhelming response. When the number of educated youths are inflating in the country by leaps and bounds, who are aspiring for getting gainful employment, it will not be in the fitness of things to squeeze employment potentiality by the application of V.R.S. with no substitution by way of denying fresh appointment. Otherwise, it will have tremendous ill effects on the society. V.R.S. should not be made compulsory for all the employees in general working in establishments. From the pragmatic point of view, V.R.S. should aim at retiring only the de-motivated and inefficient employees aged above 50 and replacing them with fresh hands. V.R.S. should also be made as an exit option to people who do not want to work any more. The objective of the scheme should not be to reduce man-power but improve its quality by infusing fresh blood without increasing its payroll cost to be able to match the new generation. This way of application of V.R.S. will weed out the unproductive and inefficient employees from the establishments and increase the efficiency in the working system with new blood who would be working side by side with the efficient employees even crossing 50 years of age.

Q. 9. Will it be in order to put an employee on probation for a period of 12 months?

Ans. An employee who is put on probation on appointment is against permanent vacancy. On successful completion of probationary period, the employee is confirmed in his services. The purpose of putting the employee on probation is to gauge his working before confirmation.

As per labour law, an employee either he is appointed on training or on probation is eligible to claim permanency in his job after completion of 240 days of working and in this case he does not need to complete 12 months of training/probation. Therefore, it will be in the fitness of things if the training/probationary period is fixed initially for six months with provision for extension of the period by another three months.

As a good employer it is always better to stick to the labour laws in toto in all respects and any deviation from the same may lead to problems and complications.

Q. 10. Will it be in order on the part of an employer to allow an employee to sign documents as authorised signatory without issuing any appointment letter to him?

Ans. An employee can of course sign many documents on behalf of the Company on instruction from the higher Management provided appointment letter has been issued to him. An employee in service on permanent cadre has to be issued appointment letter. Otherwise, his appointment in the organisation cannot be regularised as an employee on permanent cadre and in this case also he cannot sign documents on behalf of the company because of absence of his locus standi as employee in the company.

Q. 11. Can the services of a confirmed employee be terminated if he takes unauthorised leave after expiry of sanctioned leave?

Ans. Absence from duty unauthorisedly by a confirmed employee after expiry of his sanctioned leave is no doubt a misconduct on his part, but on this ground his services cannot be terminated, as per the ruling given by the Allahabad High Court. The erring employee cannot be denied the right to explanation or an opportunity of hearing in the event of his being removed from services for taking unauthorised leave. Justice S.N. Srivastava of Allahabad High Court gave the ruling on a writ petition filed by M/s. DCM Limited, Ghaziabad.

Q. 12. What is B.I.F.R.?

Ans. One of the most important legislations dealing with industrial sickness is SICA (Sick industrial companies (Special Provisions) Act, 1985) which provides for the establishment by the Central Government of a Board for Industrial and Financial Reconstruction (BIFR). BIFR consists of a Chairman and not less than two and not more than fourteen members.

When any company becomes sick it is put on BIFR. After inquiry if BIFR is satisfied that the company is unable to recoup the accumulated losses within a reasonable time, the Board feels expedient in the public interest to adopt certain measures for improving the performance of the company and in such case it may direct any operating agency to prepare a scheme providing for such measures as expeditiously as possible but within a period of ninety days. After consideration of all the relevant facts and circumstances if the company/industry is not likely to be viable in future, BIFR refers the matter to the High Court with its recommendation to wind up the sick industrial company in accordance with the provisions of the Companies Act, 1956.

Q. 13. What is the difference between lay-off and retrenchment?

Ans. Lay-off as defined in Section 2(kkk) of the Industrial Disputes Act, 1947, broadly means the failure or inability of an employer to give employment to a workman whose name appears on the muster rolls of the industrial establishment, on account of shortage of coal, power or raw materials or accumulation of stocks or breakdown of machinery or natural calamity or any other connected reason. Lay-off is temporary and is different from retrenchment, as defined in Section 2(oo) of the Industrial Disputes Act, 1947, which otherwise implies termination of service.

During the period of lay-off, the workmen concerned are not required to work but are entitled to compensation as per the provisions of Section 25C of the Industrial Disputes Act.

However, they may be retrenched in terms of Section 25P of the said Act after the first 45 days of lay-off.

An employer coming within the purview of the Industrial Disputes Act cannot resort to lay-off at its sweet will. It has to obtain prior permission of the appropriate government or such authority as the government may specify before laying-off a workman (other than a badly or casual workman).

Q. 14. Is it in order to terminate an employee without assigning any reason during the period of probation?

Ans. The fact is that a probationer cannot claim to be a permanent employee till such time he is confirmed in his services, although a probationer is appointed against a permanent vacancy. If, however, the Management has to dispense with the services of a probationary employee, it will be in the fitness of things and an act of genuine labour practice to issue him a letter asking him to be more particular in the discharge of his duties during the extended period of his probationary service by another three months or so, as stipulated in the letter of appointment. This means that he is to be given chance to improve upon his performance during probation and that the union leaders will also be satisfied that by such letter the Management has given opportunity to the incumbent to improve upon his working before he is confirmed. Even if his performance is not found satisfactory during the extended period of probation, his services may be terminated. In this connection, it is pertinent to mention here that in the letter asking the probationary employee to improve upon his performance, the Management has to mention specifically the shortcomings in the discharge of his duties, without which the letter in question will not stand.

Q. 15. If a probationary employee is not issued letter confirming his services after completion of his probationary period/s, is it correct to assume that such employee is still on probation?

Ans. When the concerned employee has successfully completed his probationary period/s, he is automatically confirmed in his services from the next date of expiry of probationary period/s, even if letter confirming his services has not been issued by the Management. However, in order to make the service records file of the employee complete and up-to-date, it is necessary that such letter has to be issued at a later date also, if it was not issued immediately on completion of his probationary period/s.

Q. 16. Can the services of a confirmed employee be terminated without assigning any reason?

Ans. Termination of services of a confirmed employee without any cause or reason and also without adhering to other formalities i.e., holding of domestic enquiry, is completely arbitrary and a breach of the principles of natural justice. If the service contract attracts the provisions of the Industrial Disputes Act, 1947, it will be an industrial dispute in terms of the said Act whereupon the Industrial Tribunal will adjudicate the same. Otherwise, the terminated employee may challenge the dismissal by way of a writ petition before the High Court.

Q. 17. If an employee meets with an accident while on duty on Company's job and is not likely to resume duty within 15 days or more, will he get salary for the number of days of his absence on medical ground and also the reimbursement of the expenses incurred for such medical treatment?

Ans. One of the terms of appointment in the private organisation is that an employee is entitled to get full or half reimbursement of salary for a certain period of his absence on normal medical ground. But, if the terms of employment of the organisation is silent in providing payment of salary to the employee in such case, the company would be bound to pay salary during the period of his absence on medical ground till recovery. This is for the specific reason that the employee had met with an accident during the period of his working on Company's job—whether at site or outside on travelling i.e., on way to reporting to duties or otherwise.

With regard to reimbursement of medical expenses, unless otherwise the employee is covered under any Act or is liable to be paid by other agency, the company has also to reimburse medical expenses to such employee.

Q. 18. Supposing, an employee has already completed 6/9 months probationary period/s as per the terms of appointment letter but no letter of confirmation has been issued to him by the appointing authority after completion of probationary period/s. In such circumstances, can the employee tender resignation without giving one/three months' notice, as the case may be, which a confirmed employee is required to do after confirmation of his services?

Ans. It is an admitted fact that if an employee could complete the probationary period/s as per the terms of appointment letter, he is automatically confirmed in the post, although no letter of confirmation has been issued to him by the appointing authority. But, in the absence of any letter of confirmation, an employee could surely tender resignation without giving any notice period for taking up employment elsewhere, for the very specific reason that non-issuance of letter of confirmation after successful completion of probationary period by the employee is the fault on the part of the appointing authority and in such case the Management has to accept the resignation without claiming any notice pay, although he is a confirmed employee without letter of confirmation. In fact, the employee has to get documentary evidence of his confirmation by way of a letter.

Q. 19. In order to prove allegation and misconduct levelled against an employee it is the Convention that domestic enquiry is held. If the misconduct is proved in the domestic enquiry without giving any opportunity to the delinquent to defend himself and also without furnishing copy of the proceedings of the domestic enquiry to the erring employee, is it correct to dismiss him?

Ans. The Enquiry Officer in his enquiry report never suggests punishment to the erring employee by way of dismissal, but mentions that the allegations and misconduct levelled against the employee have been proved. Dismissal of an employee is an extreme punishment taking into account the gravity of the misconduct committed. In the instant case, although the misconduct is proved in the domestic enquiry and if it is not a gross misconduct, the punishment warranted should not be dismissal.

In the domestic enquiry the delinquent has to be given all opportunity to defend his case by allowing him to engage his own expert in labour matters for examining and cross examining the Management's witnesses. When it is not done, the maximum punishment of dismissal is also void.

Another important aspect is that after completion of the enquiry proceedings, copy of the enquiry report of the Enquiry Officer should also be given to the erring employee. If it is not done, it is an unfair labour practice.

Under the circumstances, the employee is within his absolute right to challenge the decision of the Management to dismiss him by way of writ petition in the High Court having jurisdiction in the matter. If the employee succeeds in the case, although the chance is extremely fair, he will be reinstated in his post with back wages.

Q. 20. What is meant by sickness of a Unit?

Ans. In usual term a sick unit is that unit which is not healthy. In the eye of an investor it is the unit which has gone beyond the capacity of giving dividends. An industrialist opines that it is the unit which is suffering financial loss and is on the verge of closure. As per the Reserve Bank of India, an industrial unit is considered as sick when it has incurred financial loss for the past one year and it is likely to continue to incur the loss in the next two years also. This definition of Reserve Bank of India is applicable for the registered Companies only which has been operating business for at least seven years.

Q. 21. What are Holding and Subsidiary Companies and what is the difference between the two?

Ans. When a Company has control over another Company, it is known as a Holding Company and the company so controlled by the Holding company is called a subsidiary company.

The analyses of the Subsidiary Company are as follows:

(i) When the composition of the Board of Directors of the Company is controlled by another Company, it is a Subsidiary Company.

(ii) When the majority of the shares of the company is held by another company, it is a Subsidiary Company.

Q. 22. What is Memorandum and Articles of Association and what is the purpose of it?

Ans. For the purpose of floating a Company, the promoters of the same are required to draw up a Memorandum and Articles of Association, mentioning therein the name of the Company and determining the location of its registered office. This Memorandum and Articles of Association is to be submitted to the Registrar of companies for the purpose of getting the company registered with him. Once the company is got registered, it becomes a legal entity. The Memorandum and Articles of Association is a very important document of the company, because it contains the fundamental conditions upon which the Company is got incorporated. The Memorandum and Articles of Association is required to be drawn up in case of a Public Limited Company or a Private Limited Company.

Q. 23. What is the difference between a Public Limited Company and a Private Limited Company?

Ans. A Public Limited Company is formed by a minimum of 7 (seven) subscribers and there is no maximum limit to the number of shareholders. A foreign national or a non-resident Indian can also be a shareholder subject to the approval of the Reserve Bank of India. Having wide membership by a Public Limited company, a number of regulatory provisions are made under the company law to exercise control over the working of such Company.

A Private Limited Company is formed by a minimum of two members with a maximum of 50 (fifty) members. Its shares cannot be transferred freely. Such a Company is also prohibited from inviting the public to subscribe to its shares or debentures. Private Limited companies are, however, not subject to all the regulatory provisions which are applicable to Public Limited Companies.

Q. 24. What is meant by 'Industrial Relations'?

Ans. The term, 'Industrial Relations' has no precise definition. However, the inner meaning of 'Industrial Relations' is the interaction between employer and employees, employees and employees, employers and employers and also between the state employers and employees. Industrial Relations are an integral aspect of social relations emanating from employee-employer interaction. The Industrial Relations deal with as to how the employees get on together at their work place, what difficulties are faced by them, how is the relation with the employer pertaining to salary/wages and working conditions and how the organisations are keen to protect the interests of the employees.

Q. 25. What are the causes of industrial disputes?

Ans. There are a number of causes of industrial disputes. A dispute may be caused by any one or more of the following factors:

(a) Industrial dispute may be caused arising out of the demand of the employees/workmen for higher bonus on the ground that the organisation has been making substantial profits and the Management is depriving the employees/workmen from paying profit sharing bonus,

(b) Labourers generally want healthy and congenial working environment apart from good dealings with the Management. But, if the Management does not care for the human factor, conflict between the employer and the employees is bound to develop,

(c) When automation leads to retrenchment of employees, it is likely to cause a dispute,

(d) Demand for higher salary/wages is one of the most important factors of industrial dispute, when the employees feel that their salary/wages are not commensurate with their output of work,

(e) When the salary/wages are not sufficient to provide for a reasonable standard of living of the employees, conflict starts developing,

(f) When the salary/wages and other allowances are lower than those of the employees/workmen of other comparable enterprises, there is the dispute between the employers and the employees,

(g) When there is no job security of the employees/workmen in the enterprise arising out of the sporadic retrenchment/dismissals, the employees urge the Management to protect job of the employees and dispute is caused in the event of paying scant attention by the Management in the matter of upholding job security,

(h) When there is no congenial working condition, such as length of working hours, interval and frequency of leisure, physical work environment, safety measures and the like, dispute is bound to arise,

(i) When the Management does not pay any heed to maintain labour welfare, such as canteen facilities in the establishment employing more than 250 workmen, rest and recreation facilities, accommodation facilities for the workmen staying at a distance from their houses, washing and bathing facilities, arrangement for drinking water, health services including occupational safety, arrangement for prevention of fatigue and any other matters of labour welfare, industrial dispute is caused,

(j) In the absence of effective personnel Management, grievances and unrest which could be solved at the nascent stage, disputes also spark off.

These are the important factors which lead to industrial disputes.

Q. 26. What are the ways and means to resolve the industrial disputes?

Ans. It is always desirable that industrial disputes are not allowed to surface in the interest of ensuring running of an establishment trouble-free, taking in view that prevention is better than cure. For this, the measures like good personal Management, cordial employer-employee relationship, participation of labour in Management, good employer-employee communication system, proper understanding of the situation by both the parties, mutual respect for each other's rights, proper discharge of the responsibilities by both the parties, etc. are very important to avoid industrial disputes.

There are statutory and non-statutory methods to settle industrial disputes. When the Management and the employees' representatives sit together across the table without third party interference for settling the disputes, it is termed as non-statutory method.

If the non-statutory method, i.e. the bipartite settlement of the industrial disputes becomes a failure, such disputes are referred to the conciliation officer of the concerned state government for adjudication of the disputes. This is termed as statutory method of settling industrial disputes of an establishment.

Q. 27. Can any employer deny granting of maternity leave to a married woman employee?

Ans. Entitlement of maternity leave by a married woman employee in the event of her pregnancy and after child birth covering three months with full pay is as per statute, as there is a legislation titled 'Maternity Benefit Act, 1961'. Many organisations may, however, be outside the purview of that statute but have their own policy for maternity benefits which includes granting of leave.

Such being the circumstances, whether the Company has maternity benefits as per the statute or not, it is obligatory to extend this benefit by the Company to the married woman. Any denial of granting the maternity benefit/leave will be in contravention of the terms of employment of the organisation.

Q. 28. If the action taken by a Manager is not liked by the employees in general, what is the course left for him?

Ans. It is of utmost necessity that the Manager has to think twice before taking any action/decision, because he must be in the know that every action has reaction and this reaction may be detrimental to the interest of the employees. Taking of any action/decision hastily is never recommended and the Manager has to be meticulous in the matter. If the employees show resentment/consternation over such action of the Manager, it will of course not be in the fitness of things to rescind the decision, else it will speak ill of the competence of the Manager.

For the purpose of upholding strong administration he cannot yield to the pressure of the employees who want to dictate terms over his action.

In order to avoid sordid atmosphere in the office over such issue tactful handling of the matter by the Manager is the immense necessity. But how? First of all, the Manager has to bring the employees into confidence. They should be impressed upon that such decision had to be taken by the Management at the instance of few of the nagging employees and, therefore, for the sake of upholding administration in the organisation taking of such action/decision was felt a necessity. But, in any case the interest of the employees who are sincere and loyal to the organisation will not be affected and the Management will take care of the same. The Manager has also to impress upon the employees that taking such action/decision from time to time is necessary for upholding administration in the organisation, which is also common to all organisations. In this way, the consternation/agitation of the employees could be tamed by a successful Manager.

Q. 29. If the employees are over burdened with work, will it increase their efficiency?

Ans. Every employee has certain capacity to bear load of work. Constant pressure with heavy load of work will surely decrease efficiency of the employees in the long run and that they will not be able to work with perfection. Employees are appointed to work and not for whiling away time for inadequacy of work.

On account of lesser work the employees will be lethargic in consequence of which they will prove themselves inefficient.

Therefore, it will not be in order if the employees are either over burdened with work or they are not with less work. In both the cases, the employees cannot attain efficiency. At times, due to exigency of circumstances the employees may be over burdened with work. But this will be a temporary phase. A Manager has, therefore, to see that the employees are distributed work in such a way that they can systematically complete their allotted work without accumulation.

It has been observed that in many cases, a Manager gives constant pressure of work to the employees who are efficient. This is not correct. For shouldering heavy load of work constantly, as allotted by the Manager, the employees will be rendered inefficient in due course of time.

Q. 30. In what way the Managers are for 24 hours service of the organisations?

Ans. Managers are the pillars and magnates of organisations. Their services are unlike those of the general category of staff members who have fixed working hours in the office. The contributions of Managers lead to the efficient running of the organisations. In fact, in all respects they are part and parcel of the highest echelon of the Management and that they are always at their beck and call. Even after working hours they are not to be inalienated from the working of the organisation. Many a times the Managers continue to talk with the higher Management on phone from their residences on policy matters of the organisation. This indicates that even after their working in office they cannot shirk from their responsibilities. Managers are not workmen within the purview of Industrial Disputes Act. This is also another factor why they cannot cling to fixed working hours. Moreover, their functions are as such that they cannot wash their hands of the responsibilities they shoulder which require long hours of working. At emergent situation of the organisation, their presence is also called for even at the odd hours of night. This way the Managers are for 24 hours service of the organisation.

Q. 31. Contribution to the Provident Fund by the employees is a statute. When it is so, is it obligatory that the candidates appointed on regular basis after post-retirement service should also contribute to provident fund?

Ans. Instances are plenty that candidates even after their superannuation from the same organisation or from other organisations are appointed on regular basis, if they are found quite hale and hearty and efficient. In such case, it is not obligatory that such employees should also contribute to provident fund, because the superannuated employees after their fresh employment are not liable to be the members of provident fund and hence it is not a statute that they should contribute to the provident fund.

In this connection, it is to be noted that it will not be in order to appoint such hands in regular service of the organisation but in contractual employment and in such position those hands will get allowance only without getting any other financial benefits and not salary, as salary is drawn by the employees who are on regular service only. Candidates engaged on contractual service are not treated as the employees of the organisation.

Q. 32. Supposing, in the enquiry proceedings an employee has been exonerated from the charges levelled against him and accordingly he has been allowed to resume his duties and the management has paid him all the dues to him which were withheld during the period of suspension. (During the period of suspension an employee is only to get subsistence allowance). After the employee resumed his duties he has not been alocated any work by the management and he has been kept idling away in the office for want of work. Now, the question is—can the management act like this?

Ans. When the charges framed against the employee could not be substantiated in the proceedings of domestic enquiry, it is the discretion of the management whether to allot work or not to the employee after he resumes duties and the employee concerned cannot compel the management to allot him work. Non-allotment of work to the employee is due to the fact that since the charges levelled against the employee have been nullified in the proceeding of domestic enquiry, it has become a rebuff to the management and it may be the stratagem of the management to get rid of the employee as he is likely to relinquish his services with the company being humiliated for want of any work in the company.

Q. 33. What is the justification that the Management should not send registered A/D letter to a delinquent employee at his house putting it in an envelope?

Ans. There is always the probability that a delinquent employee can deny receipt of letter addressed to him when it is put in a registered A/D envelope. The reason which he may adduce is that he has received only the envelope without any letter inside, under the circumstances, the Management has again to deliver to him copy of the same letter when the delinquent employee reports on duty, which will not strengthen the case when the management wants to take any action against the employee. Any letter of charge-sheet has to be issued by the management maximum within two days of committing the offence by the employee. But, if receipt of such letter of charge-sheet is denied by the employee on account of the above reason, the management may be put in a bit embarrassing position. Management will, therefore, be in safe position if inland registered A/D letter is despatched to the delinquent employee and in that case the employee will not find any ground to deny receipt of such letter.

Q. 34. Should a Manager consider appointing a candidate who was once working or is presently working with the competitor's organisation?

Ans. It will be in the fitness of things if a Manager avoids appointing a candidate who was once working or is presently working with the competitor's organisation. The reason is that such candidate must be owing allegiance and/or maintaining cordial and informal relations with his erstwhile or present organisation. Therefore, there is risk always that he is likely to pass on confidential information and so such employee will be harmful for the organisation. Under the circumstances, it will be wise if such candidate is not considered for re-appointment even though he is found quite suitable for the post.

Q. 35. It is very important for a Manager to maintain sweet employee-employer relations. What are the benefits out of it?

Ans. Sweet employee-employer relations benefit both the employees and the employers. Employees tend to have more inclination to work for the organisation treating it as their own which leads to efficiency in the running of the organisation. This inclination to work depends upon the recognition of the services of the employees by the management and satisfying them in the matter of fixation of proper salary and other fringe benefits so that the employees could work with free mind and without thinking of financial stringency. Efficiency in the working of the employees is achieved when they are satisfied having cordial employee-employer relations. By such efficient working of the employees the organisation naturally forges ahead of prosperity. Troubled organisation is a sign of degeneration which can be arrested by maintaining sweet relations with the employees. Therefore, sweet and cordial employee-employer relations are the essence of benefits for both the employees and the employers.

Q. 36. It is important for a Manager to know what is ideal work environment. Ideal work environment is defined as follows:

Ans. Ideal work environment is very important to attain prosperity by any Company. Ideal work environment denotes as under:

(a) Cleanliness in the office,

(b) Better working condition,

(c) Better salary to the employees which inspires them to work more,

(d) Right job for the right employees,

(e) Punctuality in attendance,

(f) Full devotion to work by the employees,

(g) No gossiping by the employees leaving the place of work,

(h) Pin-drop silence in the office,

(i) All officers and employees have to speak in decent way,

(j) Obedience to the superior officers.

Q. 37. If any employee is not sincere to his duties and keeps the work in arrear what should be the course of action the Manager has to take?

Ans. Depending upon the extent of laxity of work done by the employees, the Manager should take action like—

(a) He should issue letter of warning. Even after receiving the letter of warning, the employee does not amend, his annual increment should be stopped by issuing a final letter asking him to be very particular in his working in future.

-OR-

(b) He should be made to understand by sweet words that his growth in the organisation is in his own hands and so he should work in the company with utmost sincerity in his own interest.

-OR-

(c) He should be transferred to other branch of the company as punishment. This course of action should be taken when the employee is beyond rectification.

Q. 38. In what way a Manager of a company can increase the working efficiency of the employees?

Ans. (a) If any employee commits mistakes in his working, he should be advised in a mild way as to in what way the work could be done precisely.

(b) The Manager should exhort and encourage the employees to do work and should not show red eyes to them if they commit mistakes in their working.

(c) A Manager should be approachable always by the employees.

(d) The employees who are working with sincerity should be rewarded by way of good increments/ex-gratia/payment/promotion.

(e) A Manager should look at the personal difficulties of the employees and give them some financial assistance to tide over their problems.

(f) The employees should be made to feel that they are inseparable from the company and that they are not working merely for the sake of monthly salary.

(g) During the course of working a Manager should also discuss official matters with the employees—but not of course in all the cases. By such discussion the employees will feel more attached to their working.

If all these tactics are adopted by the Manager efficiency in the working of the employees is bound to increase.

Q. 39. If some of the employees/workers are not willing to do overtime as per the directive of the Manager what will be the course of action to be taken in the matter?

Ans. On account of break-down of machinery in the factory or for increasing the targetted production or for keeping the pending work up-to-date, the employees/workers are supposed to do overtime work on overtime payment which is a part of their duty, as recommended in the labour law. Therefore, the employees/workers cannot refuse to do overtime work as per law, if it is within the permissible limit of overtime hours. Under such circumstances, the Manager within his right can ask the employees/workers to do overtime work. In spite of the fact, if the employees/workers are not willing to do overtime work, the Manager should issue show-cause notice to them before taking disciplinary action in the matter. But, the best course of action will be to talk to the Union leaders, if there is labour union in the organisation, so that good sense prevails upon the employees/workers not to refuse to do overtime work in future. It is not of course wise to incite the employees/workers by taking tough line of action on such issue for maintaining peace in the organisation.

Q. 40. If an employee is very irregular in his attendance and remains absent from duty every now and then, what action is required to be taken by the Manager against such employee?

Ans. Irregular attendance as well as remaining absent from duty every now and then on the part of an employee is a misconduct. Such employee spoils the discipline of the organisation. There is also probability that other employees may follow suit. Under the circumstances, it necessitates to take disciplinary action against the erring employee. Such employee has to be warned in writing to improve upon his attendance if verbal advice fails to rectify him. Even if he does not amend his ways, his annual increment has to be stopped. But, in this case he has to be informed by a letter the reason of stoppage of his annual increment. Still if he continues to act in the same way and is beyond rectification, pressure tactic is to be exerted on him, so that he starts feeling that his days are numbered in the organisation which will prompt him to see service elsewhere.

If the employee continues to remain absent from duty without information and/or sanction of leave for more than seven days at a stretch, it is a gross misconduct on his part. If the employee has formed the habit of remaining absent from duty unauthorisedly he is liable to be dealt with strongly as per law. For taking disciplinary action against him he is to be issued charge-sheet to explain his position and if the reply of the employee to the charge-sheet is not found satisfactory, domestic enquiry is to be held. If he is found guilty of the offence committed by him in the enquiry, appropriate punishment has to be inflicted upon him. It should be noted that dismissal from service is an extreme punishment which may be avoided by inflicting other exemplary punishment in such case. In this connection, it is pertinent to mention here that commission of minor mistakes of similar nature becomes a gross misconduct on the part of an employee.

It is advisable that the management should always remain on the safe side in dealing with the erring employees by sticking to the principles of labour laws, so that the union leaders do not find fault with the management in their action.

Q. 41. What is Turnaround Management?

Ans. It is essential on the part of a competent Manager to know what is Turnaround Management. Turnaround

Management refers to certain management measures which are taken by the higher management for the purpose of rejuvenating an organisation. The measures are:

(a) Management factor

Managerial inefficiency is a very important reason creating problems for an organisation. Therefore, it has been felt an imperative need to improve the quality of management. For this purpose, the higher management appoints an efficient Chief Executive Officer who has to streamline things and change the organisational culture.

(b) Financial management

It is the inevitable part of Turnaround Management to arrange additional finance, setting of financial discipline as also financial restructuring.

(c) Marketing strategy

Several organisations have to face many problems in absence of their marketing strategy. Evolving proper marketing strategy helps improve the position. Marketing strategy includes the following:

(i) Entering into new markets,

(ii) Withdrawing from certain markets,

(iii) Developing markets and new customers.

(d) Production facilities

Modernisation and improvement of plant and machinery are an important part of Turnaround Management. The measures are aimed at achieving uninterrupted production, better capacity utilisation, quality improvement, avoiding wastage and increase in productivity thereby reducing cost of production.

(e) Human resource factor

In respect of Turnaround Management human resource is also one of the important factors which includes the following:

(i) Surplus manpower should be done away with,

(ii) Morale of the employees should be boosted,

(iii) Quality of manpower should be improved through training and recruitment of competent people especially for key positions.

(f) Miscellaneous Turnaround Management

Miscellaneous Turnaround Management includes disposing of useless assets, closing down of some of the divisions/business, better management or procurement of raw materials and controlling emoluments of the employees.

The above are the ingredients of Turnaround Management which if properly implemented can ensure viability of any organisation.

Q. 42. If an employee submits resignation either with immediate effect or with effect from a subsequent date, which has been accepted by the Management and if the employee withdraws it by a letter subsequently, should the management consider his letter of withdrawal of resignation?

Ans. After submitting letter of resignation by an employee, if it is accepted by the management, the request of the employee by a letter for withdrawal of his resignation may not be accepted, because after accepting the resignation it is the discretion of the management whether to give due consideration of the letter of withdrawal of resignation of the employee or not. On the other hand, if the management has not accepted the resignation immediately and the employee has requested the management by a letter desiring to withdraw his resignation, the management will not find any ground to accept his resignation and in this case the original letter of resignation of the employee will be nullified.

Q. 43. Can an employee submit resignation during the currency of availing of leave?

Ans. It is not proper on the part of an employee to submit resignation during the period of availing of leave. If any employee has in mind to submit resignation he has to report back on duty first after expiry of leave or after cutting short of his leave and then submit resignation. Management is not, therefore, bound to accept resignation of the employee while on leave. The employee cannot go to the court of law for non-acceptance of resignation by the management in the instant case and non-settlement of his dues in the event of his resignation submitted during the period of his availing of leave.

Q. 44. How is the life of a Manager?

Ans. A Manager is a person of nimbleness. His life is blended with both solicitude and charm. In the office he is saddled with multitudinous work spiced with problems of variegated nature and the solution of the same lies with his tactful handling of the situation. His mental acumen helps a lot to arrive at a comfortable solution of such difficult and hard task. Most of the time his mind is obsessed with tension. But, still he has to remain calm and quite. Otherwise, he will look ruffled and agitated which will be damaging his reputation as a Manager.

On the other hand, he feels exalted in the discharge of his duties being crowned with such position. He enjoys credibility when things are solved to the advantage of the organisation and feels inalienable from the higher management thus solidifying his position in the organisation and in such case he derives respect as a worthy and competent Manager. Remaining in such exalted position a Manager gets opportunity to mingle with the galaxy of intellectuals which helps broaden his mind. For his working in such position he also gets esteem in the society he lives. Since a Manager is a person of responsibility there is every reason for his vaunting that he is a worthy citizen of the country. He has to freshen his mind always for passing through tribulations.

Q. 45. What should be the criteria the Managers should consider for appointment of candidates in different positions of ministerial rank and beyond?

Ans. Quality employees are the assets of an organisation of repute which runs with utmost efficiency with the galaxy of such employees. It is a known fact that the candidates who are recommended for employment are not generally of considerable worth and such candidates are to be nullified for employment as far as possible barring aside of course in the case of such candidates who are apparently found suitable after overall consideration. The following criteria are to be taken into consideration while appointing candidates:

(a) The Manager who is an interviewer should study the candidates' character, intelligence, smartness, temperament, alertness, presence of mind, patience, gentleness, way of thinking, personality and family background.

(b) Consistent academic career is to be taken note of.

(c) It is to be observed about the candidates' capacity of proper expression of things and whether they are well behaved.

(d) Candidates are to be considered for employment possessing sound health.

(e) Whether the candidates are dynamic and have foresightedness.

(f) Whether the candidates have sense of cleanliness and good habits.

(g) Candidates who are in the habit of irrelevant and unwanted talks should not be considered for appointment.

(h) Whether the candidates have aptitude. Attitude of the candidates has also to be closely studied.

(i) The candidates must have general awareness.

Apart from the above, the following are also to be taken into account for the purpose of finding suitability of the candidates:

(i) Intelligence

(ii) Self-confidence

(iii) Overall appearance

(iv) Behavioural pattern

(v) Ability to convince

(vi) Clarity of expression

While it may not be expected of the candidates appearing in the interviews for ministerial positions to fulfil all the above, the candidates for important positions should satisfy the interviewers in respect of their competence fulfilling all the aforesaid criteria for suitability of their candidature.

Q. 46. What are the criteria to give promotion in service to the employees in higher positions?

Ans. In the government organisations the criteria for promotion of employees are seniority in service and also qualifying in departmental examinations. But, it is not so in case of private organisations where the criteria for promotion of employees to higher positions are:

(a) Capability of doing work with utmost efficiency,

(b) Development of mental faculty,

(c) Leadership quality,

(d) Length of service,

(e) Way of expression of things,

(f) Relationship with other employees and officials,

(g) Conception of ideas,

(h) Grasping power.

Q. 47. What are the functions of a Manager in general?

Ans. While a Manager has multifarious duties to perform, both inside and outside the office in view of his position, the functions of a successful Manager in general are listed below:

(a) Streamlining the work of the organization whenever it is not done in proper manner,

(b) Proper functioning of administration has got direct bearing with finance. A Manager has, therefore, to see the financial aspect directly or indirectly to make the administration viable,

(c) To devise ways and means to improve the working atmosphere of the department,

(d) Implementing the plans and programmes of the organisation,

(e) With his skill and experience he has to give proper guidance and instructions and also elicit his expert opinions for the benefit of the organisation,

(f) With his personality a Manager has to get jobs done by influencing others,

(g) A Manager has to check the progress of work of the employees under his control within the scheduled time,

(h) He should have the skill to solve problems,

(i) A Manager has to make standard correspondence with others for enhancing the reputation of the organisation and for other matters.

Q. 48. What is administration and what purpose does it play for an organisation?

Ans. Administration means the governance of any activity for straightening the irregularities and disorderly state of affairs as well as maintaining viability and system. Maintenance of sound and strong administration is very important for any organisation which wants to run trouble-free. Where administration is impaired and vacillant and/or week, everything becomes messy and it quickens the degeneration of the organisation in all respects. For lack of administration no organisation can run smoothly and it leads to disarray. Therefore, maintenance of sound and strong administration in an organisation is immense. Sound and strong administration also attracts creamy candidates for employment.

Q. 49. What are the probable reasons which lead to inefficient running of an organisation?

Ans. Probable reasons for inefficient running of an organisation are:

(a) Mass indiscipline amongst the employees which includes impunctuality in attendance, leaving the place of duty without permission thereby neglecting the duties entrusted with the employees, disobedience to the reasonable orders of the superiors and regular absenteeism,

(b) Lack of executive talent,

(c) Low output of work by the employees,

(d) Financial mismanagement,

(e) Faulty decision of the higher management,

(f) Defective planning,

(g) Reckless expenditure which can be curbed easily,

(h) Poor working condition,

(i) Dissatisfaction prevailing in the minds of the employees for unreasonable stiff attitude of the higher management,

(j) Sordid employee-employer relations.

Q. 50. When the employees are at the height of their agitation over the issues not being fulfilled by the management, what course of action is left in such circumstances?

Ans. Demands of the employees backed by the Labour Union are insatiable and it is not possible on the part of the management always to mitigate their sky-rocketing demands. Even after talking to the Union leaders across the table if nothing tangible comes out and they do not want to soften their attitude to come to terms in the matter of bipartite settlement of disputes, the only course left with the management is to give information to the Labour Directorate of the State Government by a letter apprising them of the prevailing situation. The Labour Directorate then seizes the disputes for conciliation and holds tripartite meetings for settlement over the charter of demands. The demands placed by the union leaders are then settled to the satisfaction of both the management and the Labour Union by the intervention of the Labour Directorate in the interest of maintaining peace in the organisation. If, however, there is no Labour Union in the organisation, the employees cannot be militant in attitude and their demands can be solved peacefully and easily by the management without referring to the Labour Directorate.

It is pertinent to mention here that in the event of tough and militant attitude of the employees and the union leaders, the management should not take recourse to declaring lock-out in the organisation, unless otherwise of course the situation goes beyond control in certain cases, in the interest of avoiding to sustain heavy loss to the organisation by such lock-out.

Q. 51. Is it worthwhile that labour participation in the management will be helpful for smooth running of the organisation?

Ans. Industrial peace in most of the Indian industries is seriously disturbed which is adversely affecting production on account of discord prevailing between the management and the labour union. If labour participation is there in the management there will not be of course wrangling between the management and the union and hence the organisations will run trouble-free in the interest of attaining financial viability. This is no doubt one side of the advantage of labour participation in the management.

On the contrary, labour participation in management may lead to certain problems for the higher management/ which may be as follows:

(a) When there is labour participation in the management/ they will have the tendency to have upper hand and may dictate terms over the higher management which are likely to be contrary to the interest of the organisation as a whole,

(b) As far as appointment of new hands is concerned, the management may not have their own choice taking into account suitability of the candidates to appoint personnel but may have to accede to the request of the labour management for employment of such candidates of their choice even if they are not suitable for the job,

(c) Labour participation in management means sharing of power in the running of the organisation. Accordingly, difference of opinion is likely to take place which may not augur well for the organisation ultimately.

(d) There may not be of course any immediate problem but with the lapse of time problems are likely to crop up with the consolidation of labour participation in the management.

Labour participation in the management is best suited in the case of such organisations which have lost viability mainly due to labour problems.

There are many organisations which are running most efficiently and without any trouble and the employees are very happy and are working with utmost efficiency. In such organisations labour participation in the management is not felt a necessity.

Q. 52. Is it recommended that there should be interaction between the superior officers remaining at the helm of affairs of the organisation and the staff members?

Ans. Yes, there should be interaction between the superior officers remaining at the helm of affairs of the organisation and the staff members, concept of working in establishments has completely changed in modern times. Master and servant relations are no longer there in the organisations. All employees, whether high or low, have to work in unison for the organisation and each and every employee has his own contribution to render for the development and prosperity of the organisation. If barriers are there between the superior officers at the helm of affairs and the staff members generating feelings of superiority and inferiority complex working under the same roof, sense of belongings to the organisation by the staff members will be conspicuous by its absence which will be an impediment for the development and prosperity of the organisation. Work will be speeded up if the staff members are given due importance and prestige—no matter their salaries may be much lesser than those of the officers of the company. Generation of oneness has to be created. Therefore, interaction between the superior officers at the helm of affairs and the staff members is essentially needed in consideration of the fact that all the employees are the members of the same family. By this, sweet and cordial relations between the officers and the staff members will also be maintained.

Q. 53. What are the factors determining the remuneration prospects a candidate expects at the time of appointment?

Ans. While the quality and performance shown by a candidate at the time of interview are important determining the remuneration prospects, it also depends upon four factors, such as:

(a) Market value (remuneration the candidate may get elsewhere), (b) replacement value (remuneration the employer may pay for the employee's replacement), (c) job value (the skill required for the job), and (d) contribution value (for the performance of the employee).

Q. 54. Will it be in order if the female employees get lesser salary than the male employees?

Ans. It is definitely an unfair labour practice that there should be disparity in the salary structure of both male and female employees working for the same job. In India there is constitutional right to equality. While there is little remedy for the woman employees if they get lesser salary than their male counterpart working in the non-governmental organisations, since the employees have to accept the employment on certain terms and conditions, in the case of public sector or governmental organisations women employees can institute action based on their constitutional right to equality, if there is discrimination in the matter of salary and other benefits amongst male and female employees.

Q. 55. Can any employee refuse to carry out his transfer orders?

Ans. If the service regulation stipulates that the job is transferable, the employee has to carry out the transfer orders, provided the transfer of the employee has been necessitated arising out of exigency of circumstances. If, however, the transfer of the employee is with malafide intention of the management or when the transfer is effected in contravention of service regulation, the employee concerned can go to the court of law for redressal, but in this case the employee will start experiencing uncomfortable situation to work with the organisation, as the Management will not take in good taste of such behaviour of the employee. It is also the experience that the court does not interfere generally in the matter of transfer of employees, as the management is always ready to place convincing reason for transfer of the employees.

Q. 56. What is outsourcing for an organisation?

Ans. In most of the large Indian and multinational Companies there is high salary structure for large number of junior and middle level employees. In cost effective and fluctuating economic situations these organisations generally do not want to have permanent liability of such high salaried employees and, therefore, go for outsourcing all lesser skilled employees from third party agencies for contract period of one or two years. The client organisations make monthly payment of salaries to these third party agencies who in turn give the same to their employees on pay roll of the companies after deducting provident fund and E.S.I. contributions. While making payment of salaries to the employees, the third party agencies of course take a cut of five to ten per cent of the employees, remuneration. This outsourcing of employees is no doubt gainful for the organisations which have high salary structure for the junior and middle level employees, for the purpose of widening the activity of diversification.

Q. 57. What is the distinctive function of Managing Director and Director?

Ans. The Managing Director has to play the role of Chief Executive. So, he has to perform those functions which are normally performed by the chief Executive. He is the Director in the one hand and Manager on the other. Whereas, an individual Director has no power and authority. He has to act collectively through resolutions passed at the meeting of the Board. He is the representative of the shareholders. Directors are the policy makers.

Q. 58. Many industries are engaging casual labourers for doing certain job. But, the Labour Union is raising objection in many cases to the engagement of such casual labourers saying that by this engagement the management is denying employment to the incumbents on permanent basis. Is this contention of the Labour Union correct?

Ans. Engagement of casual labourers is within the purview of the labour laws. If the job is not of permanent nature, it is within the right of the management to engage such labourers on casual basis. But, the management has to see that a casual labourer does not complete 240 days of work in a year to claim permanency in the job, for which he has to be paid off intermittently for a number of days, based on the fact that the job in which he has been engaged is not of permanent nature. If it can be established by the management that the job in question is not of permanent nature, the Labour Union cannot have any say in the matter and that they cannot pressurise the Management to employ such casual labourers on permanent basis. In such case, the contention of the Labour Union that the Management is denying employment to such labourers on permanent basis is void and not correct.

Q. 59. Can a charge-sheeted employee engage a lawyer to defend himself in the disciplinary proceedings?

Ans. To all intents and purposes, management can throw out the request of the delinquent employee to engage a lawyer to defend his case. If the prosecution officer on behalf of the Company is not legally trained, the charge-sheeted employee cannot claim to be defended by a lawyer as a matter of right. If, however, the prosecution officer is legally trained, the employee can also engage a legal professional to defend his case in the enquiry proceedings and in that case the management cannot have any objection.

Q. 60. Supposing, there was no existence of Labour Union in an organisation. But, now all of a sudden the employees formed union. What may be the possible reasons for formation of Union?

Ans. Formation of Union in an organisation is no doubt the democratic right of the employees. Indian Constitution advocates trade unionism. Therefore, if the employees form union there is nothing unusual. But, at the same time a point arises under what circumstances they thought it prudent to form union in an organisation especially when the employees did not feel it necessary to think of forming union since inception of the organisation. The reasons for not forming union by the employees earlier were attributed to the following:

(a) Sweet and cordial relations between the employees and employers with interaction with the higher management,

(b) Treating the employees—whether high or low as the members of the organisational family,

(c) Job securities,

(d) Comfortable salary structure in consonance with the cost of living,

(e) Payment of profit sharing bonus,

(f) Congenial working atmosphere,

(g) Good behaviour from the management side.

If the employees start sensing that the outlook of the management towards the employees has been changing and the security and interests of the employees are being jeopardised as also the management has started becoming unreasonable towards the employees, they then find no other way out but to resort to form union as a means of guarding their interests. These are the possible reasons as to why the employees resort to form union.

Even when the employees have formed union, the management must always be benevolent towards the employees and maintain atmosphere of complacence in the minds of the employees so that they work with zeal. After formation of union by the employees, the management has also to see that they do not become militant in their attitude at any time.

Q. 61. From the pragmatic point of view what should be the salary structure of employees?

Ans. Fixation of salary structure/gradation appropriately for different categories of employees is very important for any commercial house. In consideration of size and financial stability of organisation salary structure has to be determined so that net profit is not marginalised. Most organisations of today are passing through cut-throat competition. Hence, in order to guard against such competition proper manning in the organisation is of paramount necessity. Irrational and baseless way or fixation of salary of employees has to be done away with. Also nepotism and favourtism must not be entertained while fixing salaries. There should not be disproportion in the salaries of the employees working for the same nature of job. Otherwise, it will foment displeasure and consternation in the minds of the employees which will not augur well for the organisation. Sky-rocketing salaries of the general categories of employees are not the solution to the attainment of efficient working of the employees, as has been observed in many organisations, as desire for increased salaries is insatiable. Salaries for different categories of employees should be fixed up in consonance with the present-day cost of living index as also the importance of positions in which the employees are engaged. If liberal fringe benefits depending upon the capacity of organisations are given to the employees, it does pay in the long run and the employees will be happy.

It is noteworthy to mention here that there should not be uphill difference in the salaries of the high ranking officers as compared to those of other employees so as to avoid generation of feeling of mortification. If the higher management wants to satisfy the high ranking officers for the commendable job they have done, there are ample ways to appease them.

Q. 62. If an employee submits resignation by serving one month's/three months' notice, as the case may be, in terms of appointment letter and the employer is refusing to release him, can he join his new assignment without acceptance of resignation letter?

Ans. Without acceptance of resignation letter which is submitted in terms of agreement/appointment letter, the employee can of course take up his new assignment and the employer cannot legally prevent the employee from taking up the new job. In such case, the management at least can withhold payment of dues of the employee till such time he hands over the charges. Release letter is also not mandatory unless otherwise it is demanded by the new employer. If, however, the new employer insists upon it which is most likely, the employee leaving the organisation can impress upon the erstwhile employer to issue the same (release order) and they have to issue it especially when the employee has submitted resignation strictly in terms of agreement/appointment letter. It may be noted here that if certain charges have been levelled against the employee awaiting disposal, the management is not bound to issue release order and it will not be proper on the part of the employee to join the new concern without the release order.

Q. 63. Is it in order that the management could impose punishment to a delinquent employee on the basis of the findings of the Enquiry Officer in the domestic enquiry?

Ans. Domestic enquiry is a court where findings are arrived at to judge whether the concerned employee is actually at fault or not in the matter of charges levelled against him by the management. It is, therefore, perfectly in order that the management can act upon the judgement of the Enquiry Officer in awarding punishment to a delinquent employee if the charges are proved against him in the domestic enquiry. The Supreme Court has also laid down that where a disciplinary authority states that he has gone into the findings of the Enquiry Officer and agreed with the same, it is sufficient that the Management can go ahead with inflicting punishment if the charges are substantiated in the domestic enquiry conducted by the Enquiry Officer. There is of course provision that the aggrieved employee can challenge the orders of the management by way of a writ application in the appropriate high court.

Q. 64. If a labour court awards only 50 per cent of back wages to an employee who was reinstated from dismissal of his service on account of the principles of natural justice and that the dismissal was illegal, can he claim full back wages on his reinstatement?

Ans. The law is that the dismissed employee on reinstatement may not be entitled to get full back wages. The decision of the labour court to award 50 per cent of back wages depends upon the facts and circumstances of each case.

Prom the normality point of view, the high court will also not interfere with the quantum of back wages awarded by the Labour Court. If, however, the reinstated employee feels that it was unreasonable on the part of the labour court to award only 50 per cent of back wages, he can challenge the award of the labour court before the appropriate high court in its writ jurisdiction.

Q. 65. While it is mandatory that any public sector establishment shall have to notify to the appropriate Employment Exchange for sending candidates other than managerial and the like for filling up vacancies, is it a compulsion that such candidates are to be appointed?

Ans. It is of course mandatory under Sections 4(1) and 4(2) of the Employment Exchanges (Compulsory Notification, of Vacancies) Act, 1959 that before filling up any vacancy, any public sector establishment shall have to notify to the appropriate Employment Exchange mentioning the post, salary and qualifications, to send suitable candidates for interview and filling up vacancies. But, at the same time, Section 4(4) of the said Act clarifies that the employers are under no obligation to appoint candidates sent by the Employment Exchange, if they are not found suitable for the posts. They (employers) should of course intimate the Employment Exchange as to whether the candidates sent by them have been appointed by them or not.

As far as non-employment of the candidates from Employment Exchange is concerned, the Apex Court clarified the position in the case of *Union of India vs N. Hargopal* (AIR 1987 SC 1227).

Q. 66. In some of the companies if the juniors are promoted in higher positions superseding the senior staff members in spite of the existence of merit-cum-seniority promotion scheme in the Company, could the senior employees with long working in the organisation not getting promotions go to the court of law for discriminatory policy of the management in the matter of promotion?

Ans. The decision concerning promotion primarily rests with the superior authorities and courts seldom interfere in the decisions on promotions. Therefore, it will be a difficult case for the employees not getting promotion to move the court. There are ample cases that many employees have attained seniority by virtue of long working in the organisation but they have no merit to work in higher positions. In such case, since they do not have both merit and seniority the management cannot take the risk of promoting such employees. Under the circumstances, the management has to consider such employees for promotion who have proved meritorious although they are junior to others, especially when the promotion of an employee is felt an immediate need. Otherwise, the management has to maintain the merit-cum-seniority promotion scheme.

Q. 67. When an employee is reverted as punishment for the offence committed by him, is it worthwhile that his salary has to be reduced for the lower position?

Ans. It will not be in order to reduce salary on account of demotion of the employee for the reason that the financial benefits which he was getting during the time of his erstwhile position are not curtailed. But, while granting him annual increment, after allowing fitment, if it is felt necessary, the rate of increment should be in line with the graded increment for the position he holds after demotion. If, however, his salary has reached the last stage of the gradation of the demoted position, he should not be allowed any increment i.e., there will be sealing in his salary till such time he is in the demoted position.

Q. 68. If a dispute is taken up by an aggrieved employee with the appropriate authority under the Industrial Disputes Act, 1947 and in turn the dispute is referred to the State Industrial Tribunal, what is the maximum time limit to pronounce its award?

Ans. Section 10(2A) of the Industrial Disputes Act, 1947 provides that the order referring an industrial dispute to a tribunal shall specify the maximum time limit upto three months for announcement of award by the State Industrial Tribunal provided such dispute is connected with an individual workman. But, the Tribunal has the power to extend the time limit beyond three months on application made by any of the parties, if the Tribunal considers it expedient to do so.

In this connection, it will be noteworthy to mention here that if the employee is not getting salary/subsistence allowance during the period of his suspension, he can apply to the Tribunal for directing the company to pay interim allowance to him till the award is pronounced, equivalent to the subsistence allowance as admissible under the Payment of Subsistence Allowance Act, 1969.

Q. 69. After an employee quits employment of an organisation, can the erstwhile employer institute disciplinary proceedings against that employee on corruption charge or the like?

Ans. When an employee quits employment of an organisation there is no longer the existence of employee-employer relation and hence the employer does not have any locus standi to institute disciplinary proceedings against the ex-employee, as the charges, if there were any against the said employee, were not detected by the employer before he was released from employment. If the disciplinary action is still instituted after release of the employee, he can always approach the court for quashing the same. It may, however, be noted that the erstwhile employer at best can institute some other independent legal action against the ex-employee, even if he is not the employee of the organisation.

Q. 70. When a petition is filed by the Management in the Hon'ble High court for winding-up of a Company, can the employees intervene in the winding-up application and put their case before the Hon'ble High court to protect their interest?

Ans. It was clarified by the Hon'ble High Court of Calcutta in the year, 1983 in the case of National Textile Workers' Union, that the workers of a company could appear at the hearing of petition for winding up of the company. But, once a winding-up order becomes final, the workers will have no right to participate in any proceeding in the course of winding-up of the company. However, if aggrieved by the order of winding-up, the employees are entitled to prefer an appeal in the Hon'ble High Court.

Q. 71. Under what circumstances an employee could be placed under suspension while issuing him a letter of charge-sheet?

Ans. In point of fact, service rules of an organisation provide for suspension of employees under the following circumstances:

(a) When an employee commits grievous offence for which his attendance to duties is pernicious pending finalisation of the disciplinary proceedings, he is placed under suspension while issuing him letter of charge-sheet.

(b) Suspension order can also be issued as a penalty for offence of serious nature committed by an employee.

The suspended employee is entitled to suspension allowance equivalent to one-third of his salary so long as he remains suspended. Such employee is also asked to report in person to the concerned official daily during the period of suspension.

Q. 72. It may so happen in the office that an employee working under a departmental head is not allotted any work by him thereby putting him practically without work for which the employee starts feeling humiliated in the eyes of others, which is the result of some hitch developed with his departmental head. In such case, can the employee take legal recourse to get out of this impasse?

Ans. As far as employee-employer relation is concerned, it is entirely the discretion of the departmental head to distribute work. If an employee is not allotted work and he continues to get salary as usual, even if he is sitting idle in the office, he does not have any recourse left for him to redress his grievances against the departmental head.

On the issue of humiliation the concerned employee should try to sort out the problem through discussion with the HRD personnel or the higher management.

Q. 73. While accepting the letter of an employee for voluntary retirement by the Management, stating that the release order would follow shortly, can the employee withdraw the said letter before he is finally released under V.R.S.?

Ans. The Supreme Court of India clarified that the relationship between the employer and the employee is not terminated by the mere acceptance of the application for voluntary retirement till such time the employee is actually released from service against release order subsequently issued by the Management after the acceptance of the letter of the employee. Under the circumstances, the employee could withdraw his application although the same (application) was accepted by the Management but not released from service under VRS by the release order.

Q. 74. Can the employer of an organisation deny payment of gratuity to an employee dismissed from service on ground of moral turpitude and/or fraud/financial irregularities?

Ans. It is the usual norm that gratuity payment is made to an employee at the time of leaving the employment either on retirement or resigning after completion of five years of service, in acknowledgement of the unblemished services rendered by him to the organisation. Therefore, if an employee is dismissed from the services of a company on ground of moral turpitude and/or fraud/financial irregularities, he is debarred from the entitlement of payment of gratuity, because his services under such circumstances are not free from blemish.

Q. 75. In the event of death of an employee working in harness in an organisation, can the widow or the son, as the case may be, legally claim employment in the organisation?

Ans. It is not obligatory on the part of the organisation to accommodate the kin of an employee dying in harness unless there is rule providing employment in such case. However, on humanitarian ground the employer may consider providing employment to the kin of the deceased. There have been of course several decisions of the Supreme Court exonerating the employer from the obligation of giving compassionate employment.

Q. 76. In many organisations appointment letters incorporating therein the complete terms and conditions of employment are not given to the selected candidates before they join duties but after a few days of joining the organization—why?

Ans. It is the bitter experience of many organisations that if appointment letters incorporating therein the complete terms and conditions of employment are issued to the selected candidates before they join duties, they in most of the cases do not report for duties even after getting the appointment letters in hands for the very specific reason that such appointment letters become the bargaining point with other organisations to get employment on higher salary and other advantageous terms and conditions. In such circumstances, the organisations issuing appointment letters in advance are debarred from getting the services of such selected candidates. Therefore, many organisations resort to the stratagem of not handing over appointment letters to the candidates before they join duties, although the same are kept ready, but issue simple and informal letters of appointment asking them to report for duties.

Q. 77. Can the employer reduce pay or a contractual employee during the period of his contractual service on some extraneous circumstances?

Ans. The answer is 'No'. It will not be in order to cut pay of a contractual employee during the period of his contractual service, under any circumstances, especially when the quantum of remuneration a contractual employee gets is specified in the agreement for contractual employment. In the agreement there must not be mention of pay cut in any of the clauses.

However, the other issue relates to dispensation of his service even before he completes full term of contractual service. Normally, in all the present-day employment contracts there must be mention of exit clause, permitting both the employer and the employee to opt out without giving any reason, after putting the other party on notice either for one month or three months, as mentioned in the agreement for contractual service. Therefore, the employer can at best terminate the contractual service in terms of the agreement instead of resorting to pay-cut.

Q. 78. When a head of a particular branch is transferred to another unit of an organisation in the same position, he may be required to work there under his superior. Is it humiliating for him or derogatory to his official status?

Ans. By working under a superior in another unit on transfer, it does not speak of the derogation of official status of the official when there is no dwindling of his rank. An official may be the supreme head of a unit before transfer of his services which have been necessitated arising out of exigency of circumstances, but it does not mean that there will not be any superior official above him in the unit where he would be transferred. Transfer of his services should not be considered as punishment particularly when he has not been demoted, but transfer of his services has been necessitated in the broader interest of the organisation.

Q. 79. For the purpose of guaranteeing the social securities of the employees, how many legislative enactments are there in India?

Ans. For guaranteeing the social securities of the employees working in different organisations, the following legislations are there:

(a) Workmen's Compensation Act, 1923,

(b) Employees' State Insurance Act, 1948,

(c) Coal Mines Provident Fund, Family Pension and Bonus Act, 1948,

(d) Employees' Provident Fund and Family Pension Fund Act, 1952,

(e) Industrial Disputes (Amendment) Act, 1956,

(f) Maternity Benefits Act, 1961,

(g) Payment of Gratuity Act, 1972,

Q. 80. What are the services required for labour welfare and social security in an industrial organisation?

Ans. The services are:

(a) Latrines and urinals,

(b) Washing and bathing facilities,

(c) Creches,

(d) Rest shelters and canteens,

(e) Arrangements for drinking water,

(f) Arrangements for prevention of fatigue,

(g) Health services including occupational safety,

(h) Administrative arrangements within a plant to look after welfare,

(i) Uniforms and protective clothing, and

(j) Shift allowance (for night shift).

Q. 81. What are the obligations on the part of the employers to provide for in the factories as per the Factories Act?

Ans. The Factories Act makes it obligatory on the part of the employers to provide for the following:

(a) Rest room and a suitable lunch room in all establishments employing 150 workers or more.

(b) One first-aid box for every 150 employees,

(c) Cool and clean drinking water, latrines and urinals and washing as also bathing facilities,

(d) Canteen in establishments which employ more than 250 workers,

(e) Creches in factory establishments employing more than 50 women.

The Factories Act, 1948 stipulates that the factories employing 500 or more workers have to appoint a Labour Welfare Officer to look after the welfare of the workers.

Q. 82. After suspension order is lifted from an employee on being acquitted from the charge levelled against him, is he not entitled to get full salary and other benefits which were denied during the period of his suspension?

Ans. It is not in order that full salary and other benefits which were denied to an employee during the period of his suspension would not be paid to him on his resuming duties after he is acquitted from the charges levelled against him. In this connection, it is to be noted that the Supreme Court of India gave a ruling in a case reported in AIR 1984 Sc 380 that the concerned employee was entitled to full salary and other benefits, as usual during the period of his suspension, after he was exonerated from the charge levelled against him. Usually, 1/3rd of salary is paid to an employee during the period of suspension as subsistence allowance.

Q. 83. If a candidate is over-qualified can he be denied employment for the post he has applied, on this score?

Ans. Denial of appointment to a candidate who is over-qualified for the post beyond the stipulated academic qualification as required for the post is irrational, arbitrary and unrealistic. Higher qualification cannot be a disqualification of the candidates to get employment than what is mentioned in the advertisement. The Apex Court has also held that the candidates cannot be shut out from employment for the post having higher qualification than the qualification required for a particular post.

Q. 84. What are the criteria by which employees get job satisfaction?

Ans. Job satisfaction is a very important factor which leads employees attaining their efficiency in working and the organisation in turn is also benefitted much by getting the efficient services of the employees. Hence, job satisfaction has dual advantages. There are number of important factors by which employees get job satisfaction. They are—congenial atmosphere in the office, cordial relationship between the management and the employees, standardisation in the salary structure compatible with the cost of living index and the paying capacity of the organisation, right job for the right employees, allowing attractive fringe benefits depending upon the status of the organisation, so that the employees are devoted to work which will breed work culture and the management should read the pulse of the employees to know the reasons for their discontent in working, if any. A successful

Manager has to see that the above are implemented in the broader interest of the organisation.

Q. 85. Should there be any privacy for an employee in the workplace?

Ans. If any employee during the course of his working in the workplace wants to maintain his privacy in case of mails, e-mails, phone calls, etc. which include his private communications and in such case if the employer wants to monitor the same, the employee is debarred from taking recourse to law to protect himself from such privacy, because there is indeed no right to privacy in the workplace. In fact, there is no statute in India that treats 'privacy' as a protectable right for an employee.

Q. 86. What are the prime reasons for the labour discontent in organisations?

Ans. In the earlier ages the relation between the Management and the employees/workers was like that of master and servant relation. But, this concept has now radically changed to employer-employee relation and naturally by this concept the employees deserve fair deal from the Management on all matters.

Labour discontent breeds out of the actions of the Management such as:

(a) Depriving the employees/workers of paying them the actual profit sharing bonus,

(b) Depriving them of payment of double overtime as per law,

(c) Engaging them on longer hours of overtime work in contravention of labour laws,

(d) Unfortunately, for some reason or the other the relationship between the labour and the management has not always been in proper way,

(e) Frequent termination of the employees/workers who are on probation, as per the whims and caprices of the management,

(f) On account of wrong labour policy of the management,

(g) Dealing with the employees/workers with iron hand by the management on all matters,

(h) Discourteous attitude of the management towards its employees/workers,

(i) Extracting work from them under incongenial circumstances,

(j) Discrepancy in the salary/wages of the employees/workers doing the same nature of job.

Q. 87. What is pen-down strike?

Ans. Pen-down strike is a disciplined way of resorting to silent agitation by the employees against the anti-labour policy of the Management. Employees also go for pen-down strike when they are dissatisfied with the inconsistent attitude of the Management staff towards the employees. Pen-down strike is a pointer to the Management that they should deal with the employees in such a way that there is no deterioration in the employer-employee relations in future in the interest of efficient running of the establishment by safeguarding the interest of the employees.

Q. 88. What is the difference between salary/wages and remuneration/emoluments?

Ans. Salary/wages is that amount only which is paid to an employee for the services rendered by him in a month. This amount excludes any other financial benefits. On the other hand, remuneration/emolument is that amount which includes overall financial benefits an employee gets in an organisation for the services rendered *inter alia* salary/wages. Therefore, the amount of remuneration/emolument is much more than the amount of salary/wages.

Q. 89. An organisation may have the presence of 2/3 or more labour unions with different affiliations. All of them are claimants to be recognised by the Management. Under the situation, to which Union the Management has to recognise for the purpose of holding discussions on varied labour matters?

Ans. Although there may be presence of 2/3 or more Labour Unions in an organisation, it will not be in the fitness of things on the part of the Management to recognise all of them for the purpose of holding parleys pertaining to labour matters of the organisation. In such circumstances, the management has to recognise any one of the unions, who has the maximum number of employees/workers under its fold. In order, therefore, to gauge the exact number of employees/workers belonging to each union, the Management has to invite lists from the individual unions mentioning therein the number of employees/workers under their signatures against their names who owe allegiance to such unions. On scrutiny of such lists produced by the Labour Unions, the Management has to recognise that Union only who has the maximum number of employees/workers under its fold. While recognising the Union, the Management will call all the union leaders together and intimate to them its decision of recognition. The Management will also make it clear that while negotiating/settling issues of labour problems/disputes with the recognised union, it will be binding on the other Unions who have not been recognised and such Unions will give undertakings in writing to the Management expressing their assent in the matter of settlement of disputes with such Union.

Q. 90. Under what circumstances, transfer of an employee could be malafide?

Ans. Transfer of services of an employee is a condition of service which is also stipulated in the letter of appointment. If the service rules provide for transfer for administrative reason, the employee has nothing to do against such transfer and he has to comply with the transfer orders. If, however, service rules or appointment letters specify that the employment is location-based, in such case the transfer orders of an employee could be termed as malafide. In this connection, it is pertinent to mention that class-iv employees (white collar employees) are not to be transferred for administrative reason. Even if the services of such category of employees are required at the other end, local hands are to be appointed.

Q. 91. Taking advantage of the squeeze in the employment scenario should the employers utilize the services of their employees in whatever manner they like?

Ans. Under no circumstances, it augurs well to utilize the services of the employees derogatory to their official status. There are plenty of cases that the employees are being utilized by the employers in contravention of their job profile which is the sequel to the dismal job situation. This attitude of the management is parochial and not a healthy sign for the organisation to prosper as the prosperity of an organisation is correlated to the complacence of the employees. It is not desirable that they continue to work with dissatisfaction if they are not given due weightage to the dignity of working. An enlightened management must not nurture perception that the employees could find little opportunity to get job elsewhere for squeeze in the employment scenario and hence should not extract work from them in whatever way they like by reducing the strength of the employees in the department than what is actually required. If it is done, there is every possibility that this will give birth to the formation of labour union in the organisation where the strength of employees permits for the same (formation of union).

Q. 92. Can an employee against whom domestic enquiry is conducted challenge that the Enquiry Officer was biased and that the enquiry was not conducted impartially?

Ans. An employee is always within his legal right to challenge the unfairness of the enquiry and that he can approach the court of law to direct fresh proceedings to be conducted through another enquiry officer. But, in this case, he has to substantiate that the enquiry as a whole was not conducted in a fair manner for which the employee has to take the following actions:

(a) It is of course a fact that proving biasness of the enquiry proceedings before the court of law is difficult but still then the employee can establish some definite factual basis from which such biasness could be substantiated.

(b) Mere allegation of the employee that the enquiry officer is partial in conducting enquiry and that he is biased against him (employee) will not be a valid ground in favour of the employee.

In such case, the employee has to take objection against conducting the enquiry by the enquiry officer at the threshold and that the employee has to present the facts before the court of law that the enquiry officer was not impartial in conducting the enquiry.

The Management should, therefore, ensure that the enquiry is conducted impartially so that the employee does not get any opportunity to go to the court of law to challenge the unfairness of the enquiry.

Q. 93. Can organisations undertake compulsory retirement of employees leaving option to the employees concerned to challenge the same?

Ans. Compulsory retirement scheme can be implemented by the organisations if service rules provide for the same or otherwise administrative order in respect of rationalisation of the organisations exists. Moreover, the current trend of the decisions of the Supreme Court of India is that an employee has little scope to challenge the orders of the organisations implementing Compulsory Retirement Scheme. Under the circumstances, employers have wide discretion to identify the employees for dispensation of their services either on ground of rationalisation scheme of the organisation or otherwise there is the existence of service rules to this effect, leaving no option to the employees to challenge the orders of the management for dispensation of their services on the above counts.

Q. 94. Is it not discriminatory if difference in retirement age between the management staff and clerical staff is maintained in an organisation?

Ans. It is not necessary that uniformity in the retirement age of clerical staff and that of the management staff in an organisation has to be maintained. Hence, it is not at all a discrimination if difference exists in the retirement age between the above two categories of employees in an organisation. It will of course not be in order if there is differentiation in the retirement age of the same category of employees. The Supreme Court of India has also upheld that officers of the management staff and clerical staff are not of the same category of employees and hence difference in the age of retirement of the two different categories of employees is not unreasonable and is permissible within the precincts of law.

Q. 95. Is it obligatory on the part of an employee to obtain permission from the appropriate authorities of an organisation for prosecuting higher studies?

Ans. If there is a condition in the service rules of an organisation that the employee has to obtain permission from the appropriate authorities for prosecuting higher studies he has to abide by the same so as to enable him to be eligible for one step increment in addition to his usual increment or promotion/as the case may be when he will be successful in passing the examination.

In defiance of this service condition if the employee does prosecute higher studies, which in other ways means without the knowledge of the higher management, such employee is obviously debarred from getting one step higher increment or promotion and he cannot legally claim the same.

However, in absence of service rules to this effect in any organisation, it is not of course obligatory on the part of an employee to obtain permission for prosecuting higher studies during the course of his employment, but it is desirable to seek permission from the management to improve his academic qualification which will pave the way in strengthening his case for higher increments or promotion in the organisation in future.

Q. 96. How could the departmental Managers/heads contribute to the well organised working of an organisation?

Ans. All the departmental Managers/heads have a distinct role to play collectively in ensuring well organised working of an organisation leading to its rapid development. Wranglings and distrust amongst them must be abjured and that none of them should think of that he is superior in official position to others in the discharge of his official duties, when all the departmental Managers are at par as far as their official position is concerned. They should be unanimous in their opinion that all-round smooth working of an organization is the result of their united working through open mindedness. It may be the tendency of a few of the departmental Managers/heads to come in the limelight of the higher management by oily tongue deprecating the working of other Managers. This tendency of back biting is nothing but an opportunistic policy adopted by them. These departmental Managers/heads are not trusted upon for working in unison. Such Managers/heads of departments are not expected of contributing to the well-being of the organisation, as they hanker after their personal gains only by their oily tongue. To sum up, what is needed most is that the united working of all the Managers without any complex should be their principle for the purpose of ensuring well-organised working of an organisation leading to its prosperity and development.

Q. 97. When defalcation of Company's funds is detected against a departmental Incharge, can the employer apart from filing criminal prosecution in the court initiate departmental proceedings simultaneously against the said Incharge?

Ans. There is no legal bar on an employer to initiate and proceed with a departmental proceedings together with the filing of criminal prosecution in the court simultaneously when the charge levelled against the departmental Incharge is of serious nature. Initiation of departmental proceedings by the employer is necessitated especially when the adjudication in the case by the court is likely to be delayed and the employer can ill-afford to wait till such time in view of the fact that the case is of very serious nature and the employer wants immediate disposal of the case.

The departmental Incharge against whom the charge has been framed can, however, apply to the employer seeking postponement of the domestic proceedings till the disposal of the criminal prosecution pending in the court. If the employer is not agreeable to the request of the employee, he can approach the court by way of a writ petition and seek an appropriate injunction restraining the employer from continuing the departmental proceedings. In view of the grave charge levelled against the departmental Incharge it would appear that there are complicated questions of law, evidence and fact which need to be looked into in the criminal proceedings and as such it is likely that the court will exercise its discretion in not allowing both proceedings to continue.

Q. 98. Is the Medical Representative/Sales Representative covered under the Industrial Disputes Act, 1947?

Ans. It was enacted by the Parliament that any person employed or engaged in any establishment for hire or reward to do any work relating to promotion of sales or business (but not employed in a supervisory category) is eligible for protection under the Industrial Disputes Act and other related labour legislations such as the Workmen's Compensation Act, 1923, Minimum Wages Act, 1948, Payment of Bonus Act, 1965 and Payment of Gratuity Act, 1972. Therefore, when the Medical Representative/Sales Representative is not a supervisory staff, such employee is covered under the above statutes and is, therefore, entitled to get all the benefits as an employee. In the event of breach of any of the same by the employer he (such employee) can seek monetary compensation by way of filing civil litigation against the employer.

Q. 99. In the case of dismissal of an employee if the Industrial Tribunal gives an award holding that the dismissal orders were void and directs the employer for reinstatement of the employee with full back wages and the employer does not comply with this award of the Industrial Tribunal and files a writ petition in the High Court against the award, can the dismissed employee demand from the employer full wages last drawn by him pending disposal of the writ petition?

Ans. Section 17(B) of the Industrial Disputes Act, 1947 provides that where an award of the Industrial Tribunal directing reinstatement of any workman is challenged by the employer before the High Court, the employer is liable to pay to the dismissed workman full wages last drawn by him inclusive of maintenance allowance, if any, from the date of filing the writ petition till its disposal after the workman files an affidavit in the Court to that effect, but the payment to the workman by the employer will be subject to the non-employment of the workman in any establishment during the period of the proceedings. This is a mandatory provision.

Q. 100. If certain disputes crop up between the workmen and the Management, can the same be referred to a retired High Court Judge jointly by the Labour Union and the Management instead of referring to the Labour Court/Tribunal for arbitration and whether this arbitration will have binding force as the decision of the Labour Court/Tribunal?

Ans. In pursuance of Section 10-A of the Industrial Disputes Act the Management and the workmen by written consent can refer disputes for arbitration by any retired High Court Judge who will then submit his award after investigating the disputes to the appropriate government. Under Section 17 of the Industrial Disputes Act this award is required to be published by the government within 30 days of receipt of the award In question. Under Section 17-A the award becomes enforceable 30 days after its publication and under Section 18 the award shall be binding on the Management and the workmen who refer the dispute jointly for such arbitration.

Q. 101. What are Unfair Labour Practices (ULP) resorted to by the workmen and registered Trade Unions?

Ans. Section 2(ra) of the Industrial Disputes Act, 1947 states that "Unfair Labour Practices" means any of the practices specified in the Fifth Schedule to the Act, Part-II of the said Schedule specifies the acts which amount to unfair labour practices on the part of the workmen or their Trade Union, which are as follows:

(i) To advise or actively support or instigate any strike deemed to be illegal under the Act,

(ii) To stage demonstration at the residences of the employers or the managerial staff,

(iii) To indulge in acts of violence against any workman to obstruct him from attending work.

Under Section 25(U) of the Industrial Disputes Act, 1947, any workman belonging to registered Trade Union committing any of the above acts, duly supported by them (Union) shall be punishable with imprisonment for a period of six months or with fine up to Rs. 1,000 or with both.

Q. 102. What type of criticism the employees should expect from their Managers/senior officers when they make follies in their working?

Ans. There are two types of criticism—one is positive criticism and the other is negative criticism. Employees deserve that they are not criticised personally but their working in positive and constructive way when they are at fault. Otherwise/ they will feel down-hearted and lose inspiration to work with zeal and enthusiasm. Following are the ways as to how their working with follies is to be criticised in positive and constructive manner for the purpose of heightening motivation of the employees.

(a) In the criticism there should be full of suggestions for improving the working of the employees,

(b) While criticising, opportunity has to be given to explain the position of the employees,

(c) Criticism should centre round the benefits the employees have to derive by correcting their mistakes,

(d) Criticism should be made privately and not in presence of other employees,

(e) In the criticism there should not be words of intimidation,

(f) Criticism should be made with helping attitude,

(g) Criticism should not be ambiguous so as to avoid resentment in the minds of the employees,

(h) It is the expectation of the employees that the Managers/senior officers should be cool minded while criticising them.

Q. 103. If a probationary employee takes leave on ground of exigency of circumstances during the period of his probation, will he be confirmed in his services from the next date of expiry of his probationary period/s, as mentioned in the appointment letter?

Ans. An employee is put on probation for certain months covering probationary period/s to gauge his working capability in the post in which he has been appointed and after successful completion of his probationary period/s he is confirmed in his post. When a probationary employee is not able to complete full term of his probationary period/s because of his taking leave, it will not be in order to confirm his services from the next date of completion of his probationary period/s. In such circumstances, it will be in the fitness of things to extend the date of his confirmation taking into account the number of days of leave taken by him without pay. It is, therefore, always desirable that such a point is mentioned in the appointment letter under a separate clause.

Q. 104. Who are workmen within the purview of Industrial Disputed Act? Can their services be terminated without assigning any reason?

Ans. Section 2(d) of Industrial Disputes Act, 1947 defines an employee as workman as any person employed in any business establishment to do manual, unskilled, skilled, technical, operational, clerical or supervisory work for hire or reward whether the terms of employment be express or implied. An officer can also be a workman if his working has no degree of authority involving administrative functions. Persons who are employed mainly in administrative capacity are excluded from Section 2(d) of Industrial Disputes Act, 1947.

Services of the employees who are within the purview of Section 2(d) of Industrial Disputes Act, 1947 as defined above are not to be terminated from services straightway without assigning any reason.

Q. 105. When the High Court of a State declares that the dismissal of an employee has become illegal directing the employer to reinstate him and the employer is not paying the full arrear salary to the employee for the period from the date of dismissal to the date of reinstatement, what step the employee can take to realise the unpaid salary?

Ans. When the order of dismissal of an employee passed by the employer has been set aside by the High Court, the reinstated employee is entitled to full arrear salary for the period from the date of dismissal to the date of reinstatement, subject to adjustment of the amounts received by him, if any. In this case, if the employer is not paying him the arrear salary, the remedy would be to file a money suit/writ petition by the employee against the employer to recover the dues. The money suit/writ petition should be filed within three years of the court order setting aside the order of dismissal by the employer.

Q. 106. Can an employee refuse to carry out reasonable orders of the Management and after disobeying the same can he file a suit in the competent court of law restraining the Management to issue such orders?

Ans. In a private organisation the relationship between an employee and the Management is based on a contract. Accordingly, refusal to carry out any lawful orders passed by the Management officials is tantamount to insubordination and a misconduct on the part of the employee, for which the employer can reasonably be expected to take disciplinary action as deemed appropriate against the employee. It is an established fact that court will not interfere with the actions of the Management except in the case of removal of an employee from the services of the company, if the dismissal of an employee is void and illegal. Therefore, excepting in the case of wrongful dismissal, filing of suit by the employee *prima facie* appears to be misconceived and is likely to fail. Also the company can apply to the concerned court for quashing his suit on the ground that it is not maintainable within the precincts of law.

Q. 107. What is meant by "natural justice" and how far is it related with domestic enquiry?

Ans. The principle of natural justice has two aspects—one is that no unilateral decision should be taken by the adjudicating authority without hearing the argument of other party defending on any matter and the other is that no one can be a judge in his own cause since human instinct is to defend one's own interest.

In the disciplinary proceedings of domestic enquiry, concept of natural justice plays a vital part. Breach of natural justice in a domestic enquiry and in consequence report of the enquiry officer cannot be held good and it becomes partial and unsustainable. In such case, holding of domestic enquiry has no meaning. In this connection, it is mentioned that the court of law will not interfere with the matter even if the domestic enquiry has been conducted without adhering to the principle of natural justice, if the complaining party has not suffered in any way as a result of non-compliance with the principle of natural justice.

The defending party should of course raise objections challenging the proceedings of the domestic enquiry and report of the enquiry officer if it is conducted in violation of natural justice and the appellate authority could be informed of the same with sufficient proofs of non-compliance of natural justice. This way a domestic enquiry can be made infructuous in the event of non-adherence to natural justice.

Q. 108. It is observed that in many organisations employees getting even high salaries are not still happy. What are the reasons for the same?

Ans. In certain organisations salary structure for all strata of employees is very high as compared to other organisations. Therefore, all categories of employees getting considerably high salary feel that fixation of their salary is based on the paying capacity of the organisations where they are employed. It is an axiomatic fact that in the matter of monetary benefits it is insatiable. In view of this fact and from psychological point of view, more they get more they want and hence they remain dissatisfied with the quantum of salary they receive after they are accustomed to get such high salary with the rolling of few months.

If the employees are to work being mentally dissatisfied on account of incongenial situations under unhygienic and nasty environments as also because of the step-motherly treatment of the higher Management and under duress, even when their salaries are high, unhappiness prevails in the minds of the employees and in consequence they cannot work with right earnest and zeal and show allegiance to the higher Management.

Another important factor of their dissatisfaction is that salaries of high ranking officials of the organisations are exorbitantly high and when the employees compare the quantum of their salary with that of the high ranking officials they find very big gap in the ratio of salaries which is incompatible. Under the situation, the employees feel that they are getting negligible amount of salary as compared to that of the high ranking officials and this leads to their unhappiness.

Q. 109. If the criminal charges are framed against an employee under Prevention of Corruption Act and the case is pending for disposal in the special criminal court, can the management at the same time initiate departmental proceedings against him also in the same case?

Ans. There is no taboo within the precincts of law that departmental proceedings and criminal case against a delinquent employee cannot go simultaneously. There was a ruling of the Supreme Court of India that departmental enquiry/proceedings could proceed simultaneously with the criminal case against the employee charged with having received illegal gratification. When an employee is charged with a criminal case, he is immediately placed under suspension and there is no escape for him from dismissal from the services of the company after the case is proved against him subsequently. Under such circumstances, management wants that such an employee is removed from the services at the soonest before the case is proved against him which may take a pretty long time after the verdict is awarded by the special criminal court. Therefore, pending receipt of the verdict of the said court, departmental proceedings will be expedited to dispose of the criminal case against the delinquent employee.

However, the Supreme Court of India has alternatively held that if the departmental proceedings and a criminal case are based on identical or similar set of facts and the charge in the criminal case is of a grave nature involving complicated question of law, then it is desirable to stay the departmental proceedings till the conclusion of the criminal case by the special criminal court.

Q. 110. When the proceedings in the Labour Court or Industrial Tribunal may take a very long time to resolve an industrial dispute, is there any other way out of resolving such dispute expeditiously?

Ans. When there is perception that solution of any industrial dispute may be prolonged when referred to Labour Court or industrial Tribunal there must have alternative choice that the workman can persuade the management to go to arbitration by mutual agreement. Section 10 of the Industrial Disputes Act provides that the employer and the workmen may agree to refer an industrial dispute to arbitration of agreed person(s). Such agreement must be in writing. The arbitrator shall investigate the dispute and submit his arbitration award to the appropriate government. On receipt of the arbitration award, the appropriate government shall then publish the award in the manner it deems fit within a month thereof and such award will be enforceable between the workmen and the management on the expiry of 30 days from the date of publication of the award under Section 18 of the Act. Any violation of the award by any of the parties is punishable with imprisonment for a maximum term of six months or with fine or with both.

Q. 111. After a disciplinary proceeding is initiated against an employee on allegations of misconduct, can his services be transferred to other branch of the organisation during the currency of the disciplinary proceeding?

Ans. If it is a transferable service as per service rule of the company and the employee does not have any legitimate grievance for his transfer unless otherwise such transfer is with malafide intention or in violation of statutory provision, there is no taboo in law in transferring services of the employee even during the currency of the disciplinary proceeding against him. The court or the tribunal cannot also interfere with such transfer orders when it is issued in the interest of administrative exigency. If, however, the employee has genuine difficulty to go on transfer he may request the management to defer the transfer orders, when the management may consider favourably even at the cost of administrative problem.

Q. 112. Can the employer dispense with the services of an employee simply on the basis of a letter written to the management by him expressing his intention to resign which might have necessitated arising out of some discord developed with the management?

Ans. The letter of the employee addressed to the management simply speaks of the intention to resign from the services of the organisation rather than an actual letter of resignation. Such being the situation, there is no question of acceptance of resignation of the employee by the management. Even if the management dispenses with his services mainly with the purpose of getting rid of the employee, it will be void and illegal and it can be challenged in the court of law. It is always expedient that the language, purport and context of the letter of the employee must be taken into account when inerpreting the same and it has to be decided whether or not it amounts to actual resignation.

Q. 113. What is the difference between the words, 'resignation' and 'retirement' from service?

Ans. Both the words, 'resignation' and 'retirement' denote cessation from the services of the organisation. But in service jurisprudence the words, 'resignation' and 'retirement' have different significance. While an employee can quit services of an organisation at any time through his letter of resignation, he cannot retire at any time but after he has rendered prescribed period of qualifying service which is normally after attaining the specified superannuation age. Resignation denotes complete cessation of relationship between the employer and the employee. In the case of retirement from service, relationship between the employer and the employee continues so long as the ex-employee goes on to get the retirement benefits in view of his past services rendered to the organisation and medical benefits from the organisation's medical practitioners.

Q. 114. Can an apprentice engaged as per Apprentices Act, 1961 claim to be absorbed in the company as a regular employee after completion of the duration of the apprenticeship training?

Ans. When an apprentice who is not basically an employee of the company is engaged as per the Apprentices Act, 1961, he must have to sign apprenticeship contract with the company as required under Section 4 of the Apprentices Act, 1961. It is not obligatory on the part of the employer to absorb an apprentice as a regular employee of the Company after completion of his apprenticeship period. If, however, there is stipulation in the apprenticeship contract that the apprentice shall after successful completion of the apprenticeship training serve the company, the employer will have to engage him in the employment of the company as a regular employee.

Q. 115. Daring the course of employment when an employee has furthered his technical/professional qualifications, can he legally thrust upon the employer to promote him in higher position befitting to his improved qualifications which he has acquired?

Ans. In the service contract when there is no mention that the employee will be promoted to higher position after he has furthered his technical/professional qualifications, he cannot thrust upon the management to promote him in higher position even if he acquired further qualifications. In such case, it is purely the discretion of the higher management to utilise his services in a better way befitting to his improved qualifications. The employer can of course promote such employee taking into account his past record of service in the organisation even when there is no mention in the service contract about acquiring improved qualifications for his entitlement to promotion.

Q. 116. Can an employee claim interest on delayed payment of gratuity by the employer beyond 30 days of retirement of service/quitting the employment?

Ans. Payment of Gratuity Act, 1972 provides that the employer shall make payment of gratuity within 30 days from the date it is payable. The Supreme Court of India has also clarified that pension and gratuity are not gifts to be distributed to the employees but they are the rights of the employees. Any culpable delay in settlement and disbursement of the same must attract payment of simple interest at the current market rate. Thus, payment of interest for delay in disbursement of gratuity is a statutory compulsion and accordingly an employee can rightly claim interest on gratuity if it is not paid within 30 days of retirement from service/quitting the employment.

Q. 117. Is a Manager of a company covered under the provisions of Industrial Disputes Act?

Ans. Only the 'workman' as defined in Section 2(s) of the Industrial Disputes Act is covered under the said Act. Whether a Manager of a company is covered under the I.D. Act treating him as 'workman' is explained by the fact that the nature of duty that a Manager discharges is important. If his job is mainly managerial in nature, like taking independent decisions on behalf of the company, supervising other employees under him, etc. then, generally speaking, the Manager does not fall within the category of 'workman' and in such case, a Manager is not covered under the provisions of Industrial Disputes Act.

Q. 118. Is confirmation of services of an employee automatic after period of probation?

Ans. Although it is the contention that an employee is automatically confirmed in services after completion of probationary period, as stipulated in the letter of appointment, Delhi High Court on the contrary has ruled that there is no such guarantee of confirmation of the services of an employee even if he completes the maximum probationary period. The ruling came on an appeal against the order of a single judge bench, which upheld the decision of the Karnataka Handloom Development Corporation to terminate the services of an employee after serving him a show cause notice for "unsatisfactory" conduct in absence of letter of confirmation. The counsel of the victimised employee argued that since his client completed two years of probation, as stipulated in the appointment letter, his services should be deemed "confirmed".

The counsel also said that since the notice preceded the termination but no enquiry followed, the order was punitive in nature and, therefore, invalid. But the Chief Justice, Mr M. Katju and Justice, Mr M.B. Lokur dismissed the appeal. The bench said just because no enquiry followed the showcause, it did not mean that the termination order was punitive and nor was it invalid. The judges cited earlier Supreme Court ruling to make their point.

Q. 119. What is the stipulation in Section 22 of Sick Industrial Companies Act, 1985 under Board for Industrial and Financial Reconstruction (BIFR)?

Ans. Section 22 of Sick Industrial Companies Act, 1985 under BIFR is that it provides for suspension of any proceeding when a company is sick and is referred to Board for Industrial and Financial Reconstruction. In spite of such stipulation in Section 22 of Sick Industrial Companies Act, 1985 if an employee makes a representation to the state government under the Industrial Dispute Act, 1947 for his reinstatement with back wages for dismissal/termination of his services, which is referred to the Industrial Tribunal by the government and meanwhile the company becomes sick and is registered its case with BIFR under the Sick Industrial Companies Act, 1985, the claim of the employee for his reinstatement with back wages should not be affected by Section 22 of the 1985 Act provided the Tribunal holds in favour of the employee's case for reinstatement with back wages, otherwise, proceeding for recovery of back wages with reinstatement may be hit by Section 22.

Q. 120. What is the difference between termination and dismissal of an employee?

Ans. The words, 'Dismissal' and 'Termination' are identical as in the case of dispensation with the services of an employee. But, basically there is a distinct difference between the two. An employee who is covered under the Industrial Disputes Act, 1947 is dismissed from the services of an organisation whose misconduct is substantiated in the domestic enquiry or when he is caught red-handed while committing any offence of gross misconduct. On the other hand, services of an employee are terminated straightway without assigning any reason in pursuance of conditions of service or otherwise. Such employee is not covered under Industrial Disputes Act, 1947.

Q. 121. Can the employer of a company pay lesser salary to their female employees than that of their male employees doing similar nature of job? (Following is the alternative answer to previous answer against question No. 54).

Ans. In pursuance of Section 4 of the Equal Remuneration Act, 1976, there cannot be disparity in the rates of salary payable to male and female employees who perform the same work or work of a similar nature in an organisation. If any organisation violates the provision of the said Section by paying lesser salary to their female employees than that of their male employees doing the same nature of job, complaint could be lodged against the management before the authority constituted by the government under Section 7 of the 1976 Act. The punishment in such case could be minimum fine of Rs. 10,000 up to a maximum of Rs. 20,000 or imprisonment for a term between three months and one year or both. If the employer is a limited company, then every person responsible for the conduct of the business of the company shall be deemed to be guilty of the offence and be liable to be punished accordingly.